The Essence of Leadership

The Essence of Leadership

The Four Keys to Leading Successfully

EDWIN A. LOCKE
AND ASSOCIATES

LEXINGTON BOOKS
Lanham • Boulder • New York • Oxford

LEXINGTON BOOKS

Published in the United States of America
by Lexington Books
4720 Boston Way, Lanham, Maryland 20706

12 Hid's Copse Road
Cumnor Hill, Oxford OX2 9JJ, England

British Library Cataloguing in Publication Information Available

The hardback edition of this book was previously catalogued by the Library of Congress
as follows:

Locke, Edwin A.
   The essence of leadership : the four keys to leading successfully / Edwin A. Locke ;
  with Shelley Kirkpatrick . . . [et al.].
     p.   cm.
  Includes index.
   1. Leadership. 2. Executive ability.   I. Kirkpatrick, Shelley. II. Title.
HD57.7.L63   1991
658.4'09 —dc20   91–3705
                                          CIP

ISBN 0–7391–0054–8 (pbk. : alk. paper)

Printed in the United States of America

♾™ The paper used in this publication meets the minimum requirements of American
National Standard for Information Sciences—Permanence of Paper for Printed Library
Materials, ANSI/NISO Z39.48–1992.

The authors and the publisher gratefully acknowledge permission to reprint excerpts from the following publications:

Bennis, W. G., and B. Nanus. 1985. *Leaders: The Strategies for Taking Charge.* Copyright © 1985 by W. G. Bennis and B. Nanus. Reprinted by permission of HarperCollins Publishers.

Boyatzis, R. E., 1982. *The Competent Manager.* Copyright © 1982 by J. Wiley & Sons, Inc. Reprinted by permission.

Gabarro, J. J. 1987. *The Dynamics of Taking Charge,* pp. 11, 57, 87, 105, 117. Boston, Mass.: Harvard Business School Press. Used with permission.

Howard, A., and D. W. Bray. 1988. *Managerial Lives in Transition: Advancing Age and Changing Times.* Reprinted by permission of Guilford Press.

Howard, R. 1990. "Values Make the Company: An Interview with Robert Haas." *Harvard Business Review* (September-October), 133–44. Used with permission.

Kouzes, J. M., and B. Z. Posner. 1987. *The Leadership Challenge: How to Get Extraordinary Things Done in Organizations.* Reprinted by permission of Jossey-Bass.

Peters, T. 1987. *Thriving on Chaos: Handbook for a Management Revolution.* Copyright © 1987 by Excel, a California Limited Partnership. Reprinted by permission of Alfred A. Knopf, Inc.

*To real
and aspiring leaders
everywhere*

Contents

Foreword

We all are fascinated by great leaders. One of the greatest, Sir Winston Churchill, had insight into the quality of leadership: "I am certainly not one of those who need to be prodded. In fact, if anything, I am the prod."

That is certainly one aspect of leadership, but there are many others. One quality that Churchill possessed to a degree unmatched by most statesmen in this century was the ability to articulate a vision, to capture the essence of a situation in well-chosen and memorable words. It didn't hurt, too, that he was one of the best orators of his time, or probably of all time.

But is leadership in politics the same as leadership in business? And if it is, what is the essence of leadership?

Edwin Locke's *The Essence of Leadership: The Four Keys to Leading Successfully* offers provocative answers to these questions. This work is a valuable source of the best that has been said and written about the elusive essence of leadership. It it a timeless topic that extends from the time of the Pharaohs of ancient Egypt and Julius Caesar to today's political leaders, and can be applied to Andrew Carnegie and Henry Ford as well as to the chief executive officers of today's corporations. You are certain to find here new insights that will amuse, provoke, and enlighten, and that will enrich your understanding of one of the most important human qualities.

—Ralph Larsen, Chairman and Chief Executive Officer
Johnson & Johnson

Preface

In the spring of 1989 I taught a graduate seminar on the topic of leadership. I had never wanted to teach such a course previously, because I had always thought that what behavioral scientists called "leadership theories" were not theories of leadership at all but rather theories of supervision. Not only did such theories fail to identify what the leader or top person in the organization did, I thought, they dealt mainly with leadership "style" rather than substance. For example, there were endless debates about whether effective "leaders" had to be participative, yet a yes or no answer could not be given to this question—probably because it was the wrong question to ask. The proper question is *when* should one use participation? But more important than style is substance; we need to know what leadership actually *is* before we can know the best style in which to do it.

Fortunately, in recent years a number of books have appeared that focused on what real leaders do. These were the books that we read in the seminar. Despite the fact that these books were primarily qualitative (based on interviews with and observations of real leaders) rather than quantitative, our goal was to see whether consensus emerged as to what leadership consisted of and what made some leaders more effective than others.

It became evident quite early in the course that there was a very strong convergence among the various books. Each week during the course we built a leadership model, then revised it the next week based on the new reading. After about six weeks, we continued to refine the model, but we were learning very little that was new or fresh from each additional source. The model also made sense in terms of our own observations about leadership.

Finally, we further "verified" the model by asking two successful leaders, President William Kirwan of the University of Maryland at College Park and Stewart Bainum, Jr., president of Manor Care, Inc., to present their views on leadership. Even though they were not very familiar with the literature we had been reading, their personal views fit very well into our model.

At the end of the course, each member of the class wrote a long term paper presenting his or her model of leadership. Not surprisingly, there was a high degree of convergence among the papers despite differences in details.

At the same time it became evident that none of the books we had read had included all the parts of the model that we had developed. Where the various sources overlapped, they were in basic agreement, but each book only included select pieces of the puzzle.

Thus we decided that a new book was in order. We call it *The Essence of Leadership* to stress that it deals with essentials rather than every minute facet of leadership. Since the book is an integration mainly (although not exclusively) of qualitative studies, the model it presents cannot be taken as scientifically proven. We believe, however, that it is highly plausible. It is consonant with what people who have actually studied leaders discovered, and it encompasses themes that have emerged over and over again, in study after study. Finally, it is consonant with our own limited observations of what effective leaders do.

To make our presentation of the synthesized ideas and the model they support more readable, we have opted to state our findings as assertions of fact rather than constantly qualifying them with the disclaimers stated above.

A concluding note: Although the different chapters were written mainly by different people, I have edited each chapter numerous times (some as many as six times), and an outside editor, Joyce Case, edited the whole book. This insured both consistency of viewpoint and continuity of style. I wrote Chapters 1 and 6. The people who did the main writing of the other chapters are noted at the bottom of the first page of his or her chapter. Dong-Ok Chah was responsible for the references, figure, and index, and for contributing ideas for the other chapters.

The authors would like to express their gratitude to Joyce Case, whose excellent editorial work made this a much better book.

—Edwin A. Locke

The Essence of Leadership

1

The Nature of Leadership

There probably has never been a society, country, or organization that did not have a leader; if there has, it probably did not survive for long. The importance of leadership in the conduct of human affairs has been recognized since the beginning of recorded history.

The case for business leadership is stated by Warren Bennis and Burt Nanus as follows: "A business short on capital can borrow money, and one with a poor location can move. But a business short on leadership has little chance for survival" (1985, p. 20). This is truer today than ever before because of current factors like the increasing rate of technological change, intensifying global competition, deregulation, and the demand for faster competitive response.

Ominously, a recent *Fortune* magazine article reported that

left to guess their CEO's plan, many employees end up wondering whether the brass has one. Confidence in top management's competence is collapsing. [Vice-president of Opinion Research Ilene] Gochman found an across-the-board vote of declining confidence she calls "just unbelievable." . . . Gochman concludes that management's low ratings arise from workers' awareness of new challenges out there

—presumably combined with the belief that top management is not meeting those challenges (Farnham 1989, p. 58).

Although many of the leadership practices championed here may also be effective in political applications, the focus of this book is primarily on organizational and business leadership. There are many dramatic examples of business leaders founding new industries (such as John D. Rockefeller at Standard Oil), turning around failing companies (like Lee Iacocca at Chrysler), guiding their organizations through long periods of growth (Tom Watson at IBM, Harold Geneen at ITT, and Alfred Sloan at General Motors), and dramatically reorienting their companies' strategic postures (Jack Welsh at General Electric). The well-publicized achievements of these leaders mirror hundreds of thousands of cases of effective organizational leadership that occur daily on a smaller scale.

It was not until the turn of the century that social scientists began to study leadership systematically. One recent article estimates that there have been more than three thousand studies of leadership in the past seventy years (Schriesheim, Tolliver, and Behling 1983). Many of these studies, however, are not really of leaders but rather of supervisors, and many of them are not very enlightening. The contentions of Bennis and Nanus that "leadership is the most studied and least understood concept of any in the social sciences" and that "never have so many labored so long to say so little" is strongly supported by a perusal of the "classic" leadership literature (1985, pp. 4, 20). Yet thanks to social scientists such as those two, this picture has changed radically in recent decades. Narrow, trivial studies have been supplanted by studies of what effective leaders—not supervisors—actually do. Furthermore, the emerging picture of what effective leadership requires is quite consistent from study to study.

What Is Leadership?

We define leadership as *the process of inducing others to take action toward a common goal.* This definition subsumes three elements:

- Leadership is a *relational* concept. Leadership exists only in relation to others—namely, followers. If there are no followers, there is no leader. Implicit in this definition is the premise that effective leaders must know how to inspire and relate to their followers.
- Leadership is a *process*. In order to lead, the leader must do something. As John Gardner (1986–88) has observed, leadership is more than simply holding a position of

authority. Although a formalized position of authority may greatly facilitate the leadership process, simply occupying such a position is not sufficient to make someone a leader.

- Leadership requires *inducing* others to take action. Leaders induce their followers to act in numerous ways, such as using legitimate authority, modeling (setting an example), goal-setting, rewarding and punishing, organizational restructuring, team-building, and communicating a vision.

The contrast between leadership and dictatorship must be noted. A dictator gets others to act by physical coercion or by threats of physical force. Some dictators, to be sure, engage in certain activities characteristic of leaders, such as offering visions. (For example, Hitler inspired the German people by offering them a vision of a world dominated by the Germans; Lenin inspired his followers by a vision of a communist utopia.) But ultimately a dictator relies on force to actualize whatever vision he might have. As Mao Zedong put it, "Power grows out of the barrel of a gun." This is true of the power of dictators, but it is not true of leaders.

Some have argued that an effective leader can induce followers to transcend their own self-interest for the sake of the organization (e.g., Bass 1985). Actually, most people, unless they are cowed or brainwashed victims of communistic or other dictatorial governments or of self-destructive philosophies, do not act in the long run against their own self-interest.

A better description of what effective leaders do with respect to their subordinates is that they convince them that their self-interest lies in buying into the vision that leaders have formulated and in working to implement it. Chapters 4 and 5 discuss in more detail how a leader motivates subordinates, but we may state here briefly that basically this is done by:

- convincing subordinates that the organizational vision (and the subordinates' role in it) is important and attainable;
- challenging subordinates with goals, projects, tasks, and responsibilities that allow them to feel a sense of personal (as well as group and organizational) success, achievement, and accomplishment; and
- rewarding subordinates who perform well with recognition, money, and promotions.

Leaders can ask employees to forego excitement, success, and rewards temporarily, under emergency conditions, but they cannot do it (and get away with it) permanently, as a way of life. Leaders in the business world who foster work environments in which there are sustained deprivations find that their employees—especially the best ones—soon look elsewhere for jobs. Those who stay may go on strike or try to get back at the organization in other ways (Fisher and Locke, in press).

Leadership versus Management

Despite an ongoing dispute among writers on leadership over whether there is a valid distinction between leadership and management, we believe that the distinction is not only valid and important but also very simple.

- The key function of a *leader* is to establish the basic vision (purpose, mission, overarching goal, or agenda) of the organization. The leader specifies the end as well as the overarching strategy for reaching it (Kotter 1990).
- The key function of a *manager* is to implement the vision. The manager and subordinates act in ways that constitute the means to achieving the stated end.

In reality, as John Gardner (1986–88) has noted, this distinction often gets blurred. This is not because the distinction is invalid, but because in practice, the roles of leader and manager have no clear line of demarcation. Effective leaders must play a role in implementing their own visions, and effective managers must not only buy into the leaders' visions, they must act, in part, as leaders to those below them. High-level managers (executives) may play a role both in the formulation and the implementation of the organization's vision.

Too often, leaders perform only the managerial part of their job. Many organizations today, insist Bennis and Nanus (1985), are "overmanaged and underled" (quoted in Kotter 1990). It is widely believed that in the future, not only will leaders have to lead more effectively, but managers, to whom more and more responsibility will be delegated, will have to play a greater leadership role. In short, there will have to be more leading to give direction to the managing.

Transformational versus Transactional Leadership

The distinction between transformational and transactional leadership, two very popular concepts today, is not nearly as simple as that between leadership and management, because the definitions of these concepts are quite confusing.

- *Transformational* leadership has been defined (Bass 1985; Burns 1978; Tichy and Devanna 1986) as leadership that involves changing the organization (as contrasted with leadership designed to maintain the status quo). It has also been defined as leadership that involves motivating subordinates to work for so-called "higher-level" goals that allegedly transcend their immediate self-interest.
- *Transactional* leadership has been defined as leadership that maintains or continues the status quo. It has also been defined as leadership that involves an exchange process, whereby followers get immediate, tangible rewards for carrying out the leader's orders.

Confusion arises between these two terms with respect to the issue of change. The true opposite of transformational leadership is static or status quo leadership, not transactional leadership, since the opposite of change is no change.

With respect to defining the type of rewards offered, neither term is really suitable. There is no necessary association between transformational (change-focused) and nontransformational (static) leadership on the one hand and the type of reward used on the other.

All leadership is in fact transactional, but such transactions are not always confined to short-term monetary rewards. *All* effective leaders must appeal to their followers' self-interest, as the followers perceive it or are persuaded to perceive it. The interests in question can be short-term or long-term or both. These interests can and do involve both tangible rewards (such as pay) and intangible rewards (such as working toward a goal perceived as important). Transformational and transactional leaders use both types of rewards (Yukl 1989), and leaders who use a wide variety of both short-term and long-term rewards are more likely to be effective than those who do not.

A more important question is whether nontransformational leadership should be called leadership at all. Probably it should not. Working toward a goal implies guiding the organization toward an end that it has not achieved before, rather than repeating what has been done already. Leaders who simply do what their predecessors did are acting not so much as leaders as managers. Real leaders must take the organization, in some respect, in a new direction. This is not to say that leaders should institute change for the sake of change. Change should be a calculated response to the world that is rapidly changing. Leaders who do not anticipate this changing world, or at least respond to it, risk allowing their organizations to stagnate and ultimately fail.

The Leadership Model

This book focuses on the leadership model provided in figure 1–1, which was developed from an integration of recent works on leadership. (Most of these works involve qualitative studies of actual organizational leaders.) It consists of four key parts.

The *motives and traits* that are characteristic of effective leaders have been found to be different from those of nonleaders. Effective leaders

- are full of drive, energy, and ambition;
- are tenacious and proactive in pursuing their goals;
- want to lead—they do not crave power for the sake of dominating others but for the sake of achieving an overarching goal;
- are honest and have integrity—not only can they be trusted, but they also trust others;
- have a high degree of self-confidence, which enables them not only to undertake grave responsibilities and generate confidence in others but to cope with many potentially stressful situations with equanimity;
- are often creative;
- are strategically flexible when the situation calls for it;
- are sometimes charismatic (but this is not an essential for effective leadership).

FIGURE 1-1

Leadership Model

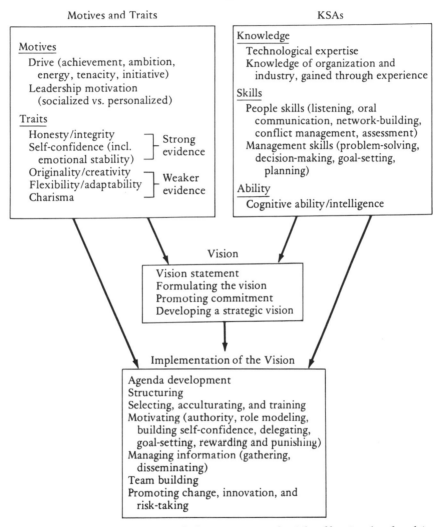

Knowledge, skills, and ability associated with effective leadership include:

- extensive knowledge of the industry, technology, and organizational environment in which they are working, typically gained from years of experience;
- a variety of skills. Because of the relational nature of leadership, "people skills" are important. These include

listening, oral communication, network-building, conflict management, and assessment of self and others. Problem-solving, decision-making, and goal-setting skills are also vital;

- cognitive ability, specifically the intelligence to process a large amount of information, integrate it, and draw logical conclusions from it.

Vision is another vital leadership component. Leaders' drive, motivation to lead, experience, and intelligence provide them with the capacity to

- define what their organizations should strive to be and to do;
- articulate that vision succinctly;
- formulate a strategic vision that specifies the means by which the vision will be attained;
- promote commitment from their followers by communicating in a manner that is both clear and compelling.

Implementation of the vision is a requirement for leadership success. A vision that is not implemented remains only a dream. The effective leader takes steps to insure that the vision is translated into specific actions, which usually are accomplished with the help of managers and their subordinates.

Effective implementation actions fall into six major categories:

- *Structuring* allows for innovation and rapid response to market conditions without interference from above. Effective modern organizations are moving rapidly in the direction of fewer layers of authority (flat rather than tall hierarchies), fewer bureaucratic rules, larger spans of control, decentralization, smaller central staffs, and smaller sized subunits.
- *Selection, training, and acculturating of personnel* is carefully monitored so that only individuals considered capable of performing effectively are selected. Focused training insures that they will understand and accept the organizational vision.

- *Motivating* subordinates is done in a number of ways by effective leaders, including

  —using legitimate authority to get people to do what is wanted;

  —serving as a role model by doing the things they want their subordinates to do (such as asking customers what they think of the company's services or products);

  —building self-confidence in subordinates by expressing confidence in them and their abilities;

  —setting specific and challenging goals;

  —delegating the responsibility and authority for attaining goals to capable managers and employees;

  —rewarding those who buy into the vision and strive to accomplish it with recognition, pay raises, bonuses, and promotions; conversely, punishing those who do not perform by withholding rewards and by termination.

- *Managing information* is another hallmark of effective leaders. They are exceptional information-gatherers. They listen to their subordinates and to sources outside the organization, especially customers. They are around and available, not remote and unapproachable. They read. They develop wide information networks. They share and disseminate information appropriately within the organization.

- *Team building* takes place at the top management level and is encouraged at all levels below in an organization run by an effective leader.

- *Promoting change* is an unwavering practice of effective leaders because of the recognition that an organization that does not change is one that does not survive in the long run. The need for change and innovation is communicated constantly. Goals for positive change are set, and rewards are given when they are accomplished. Calculated risk-taking is the norm.

What about Leadership Style?

"Leadership style," the core of traditional leadership theories, is completely missing from the model we use in this book. This is not by accident. Over and over again, people who have studied leaders observe that leadership styles (such as how much participation leaders encourage, how extroverted they are, how intense or low key they are) differ widely from leader to leader.

Where leaders do *not* differ is in substance. Effective leaders are motivated and honest. They know how to deal with people. They have a vision, and they work tirelessly to achieve it. These are the essentials of leadership, so these are what this book is about. Each of the four key aspects of leadership will be dealt with at length in the chapters that follow.

The model reveals that what are called "trait theories" (or what used to be called "great man" theories) are not totally wrong and yet are not fully adequate as theories of leadership—and why this is so. The possession of certain traits appears to be a necessary precondition for effective leadership. For example, leaders must be energetic and honest, and they must want to lead. But such traits alone are not sufficient. If leaders are to be effective, they must *use* their traits to develop skills, formulate a vision, and implement this vision in reality. Thus, traits constitute only a part of the picture.

Contingency Theory

In "contingency theories" of leadership, traditional leadership theorists commonly claimed that leadership theories have to be situationally contingent: that different leadership principles have to apply in different situations. The contingencies might involve such factors as the volatility of the environment, the size of the organization, the amount of authority given the leader, the complexity of the task or technology, and so on (Yukl 1989). Because most of these contingency theories dealt with supervision rather than real leadership, it is difficult to evaluate the validity of their claims.

Different situations may actually require different types of leaders in certain respects. The purpose of our model, however, is to present the *leadership core*: the essentials of the leadership process. If there are contingencies, they more likely involve the weight or degree of importance that should be accorded the various parts or subparts of the model rather than the core components themselves. For example, intelligence may be less important in an industry of low technological complexity than in one of high technological complexity. Similarly, experience may be more important in some industries than in others. More entrepreneurial traits might be required in beginning new enterprises (although the pace of change is now so rapid that all effective leaders have to foster change and innovation to some extent).

Some aspects of the model appear to be equally crucial for *all* leaders if they are to be effective. Desiring to lead, having honesty and integrity, dealing effectively with people, and creating and communicating a vision are important in all leadership settings. Since this model is based mostly on qualitative data, however, scientific proof of these assertions has to await empirical testing. Until then, the present model is recommended as a guideline for leaders—and aspiring leaders—to use.

Leadership Motives and Traits

Few issues have had a more controversial history than that of leadership traits. In the nineteenth and early twentieth centuries, "great man" leadership theories were highly popular (Bass 1990). The "great man" theories asserted that leadership qualities were inherited, especially by people from upper classes. Stressing hereditary superiority, the "great man" theories evolved in the early part of the twentieth century into trait theories. The trait theories made no assumptions about whether leadership traits were inherited or acquired but simply asserted that leaders were different from nonleaders in their characteristics.

The trait view was thrown into confusion at midcentury when early reviewers of leadership research came to the conclusion that there is no clear tie between a leader's traits and effective leadership (see Lord, De Vader, and Alliger 1986). Reviewers who came to this conclusion discouraged subsequent research concerning leader traits for many years. But psychologist Gary Yukl (1989) argues that when these leadership researchers concluded that traits made no difference at all, they had overreacted to the pessimistic reviews. It now seems clear that certain traits and motives do indeed influence a leader's effectiveness, although how critical to success any particular trait or motive is appears to depend on the situation. Striking an appropriate balance of emphasis is difficult, and Bass (1990, p. 78) indicates that past reviewers "overemphasized the situational and underemphasized the personal nature of leadership."

Chapter 2 was written mainly by Shelley Kirkpatrick.

A major reason for the difficulty in finding a strong relationship between leader traits and leader effectiveness is that although certain traits are necessary for effective leadership, they are not sufficient by themselves. The traits must be present in combination with other factors. Even when a leader possesses the essential traits, to be effective he or she must also possess or gain necessary knowledge, skills, and abilities and must develop and implement a vision.

Possessing the core motives and traits discussed in this chapter is a precondition for any individual to become an effective leader. The core motives are *drive* and *leadership motivation,* and the core traits are *integrity/honesty* and *self-confidence.* There is some evidence that other traits—originality, flexibility and charisma—are related to effective leadership, but evidence that they are absolutely necessary is less clear-cut than that of the others.

The Core Motives

A *motive* is a want that moves a person to action. Some motives are general, and they move people to act similarly across a variety of superficially different situations. A number of these general motives are found in successful leaders.

Drive

For lack of a better term, *drive* is used here to encompass a variety of related although not identical motives.

Achievement is one of these. High achievers typically gain satisfaction by successfully completing challenging tasks, by attaining standards of excellence, and by developing better ways of doing things (Wexley and Yukl 1984). To work their way up to the top of an organization, leaders must have a desire to complete challenging assignments and projects. This spurs them to gain technical expertise through education and work experience,. and to initiate and follow through with organizational changes.

An individual who wants to lead but who has no desire to achieve is unlikely to succeed in either creating or implementing a vision. The literature is nearly unanimous in finding that leaders have a relatively high desire for achievement (for example, Bass 1990;

Yukl 1989). Psychologist Bernard Bass (1990) reviewed twenty-eight studies and found evidence that the desire for achievement is an important motivating factor among effective leaders. David McClelland (1965) has conducted extensive research on the need for achievement and finds that it is a particularly important motive among successful entrepreneurs.

The constant striving for improvement is illustrated by the case of Tom, a manager who took charge of a $260 million industrial- and office-products division:

> After twenty-seven months on the job, Tom saw his efforts pay off: the division had its best first quarter ever. By his thirty-first month, Tom felt he had finally mastered the situation. . . . [Tom] finally felt he had the structure and management group in place to grow the division's revenues to $400 million and he now turned his attention to divesting a product group which no longer fit in with the growth objectives of the division. (Gabarro 1987, p. 11)

To perform well, a leader needs to constantly work toward success and improvement. Professor Henry Mintzberg (1973) finds that leaders and managers perform a large amount of work at an unrelenting pace. Richard Boyatzis (1982) finds that superior managers and executives are higher than average executives in their "efficiency orientation," defined as a concern with doing something better than one has done it before or better than others have done it. And at PepsiCo, only such "aggressive achievers" were found to have survived (Dumaine 1989). Tom Watson of IBM has been described as "driven throughout by a personal determination to create a company larger than NCR" (Smith and Harrison 1986).

Ambition is a second, closely related leadership motive that is encompassed by the word *drive*. Leaders must have a desire to get ahead in their careers and make their divisions and companies grow and prosper. To advance through the ranks, leaders must actively take steps to demonstrate their drive and determination. Ambition impels leaders to set hard, challenging goals for themselves as well as for their organizations, and they are typically very ambitious in their work and careers (Bass 1990; Cox and Cooper 1988; Howard and Bray 1988). Leaders are significantly more ambitious than non-leaders. According to Ken G. Smith and Kline Harrison, Walt Disney, the founder of Walt Disney Productions, had a "dogged determination to succeed" (1986, p. 27-3), and "inexhaustible ambition" is attributed to C. E. Woolman of Delta Air Lines.

Among a sample of managers at AT&T, ambition—specifically, the desire for advancement—was the strongest motivational predictor of success over twenty years. Psychologists Ann Howard and Douglas Bray provide character sketches of two managers who successfully progressed through that company's ranks.

> "I want to be able to demonstrate the things I learned in college and get to the top," said Al, "maybe even be president. I expect to work hard and be at the third level within 5 years, and to rise to much higher levels in the years beyond that. I am specifically working on my MBA to aid in my advancement. If I'm thwarted on advancement, or find the challenge is lacking, I'll leave the company."

> [Another manager] had been promoted to the district level [after eight years] and certainly expected to go further. Although he still wouldn't pinpoint wanting to be president (his wife's dream for him), he certainly had a vice presidency (sixth level) in mind as early as year 2 in the study, after his first promotion. (Howard and Bray 1988, pp. 70, 186)

By contrast, the following two sketches illustrate less ambitious individuals:

> Even though Chet had the benefits of a college degree, his below-average scholastic performance did not fill him with confidence in his capabilities. He hedged a bit with his interviewer when asked about his specific aspirations, saying he wasn't sure what the management levels were. When pressed further, he replied, "I'd like to feel no job is out of my reach, but I'm not really possessed of a lot of ambition. There are times when I just want to say, 'To hell with everything.'"

> After [his] promotion to the second level, [another manager] looked more favorably upon middle management, but he still indicated he would not be dissatisfied to stay at the second level. [He] just seemed to take each position as it came; if he ever looked ahead, he didn't appear to look up. (Howard and Bray 1988, pp. 70, 187)

Three other "motives" that are encompassed by the word *drive* can be viewed as implementing traits or behavioral manifestations of the motives of achievement and ambition. All five are grouped together here because they are so closely related.

Energy is necessary for leaders to sustain a high achievement drive and get ahead in their organizations (Bass 1990; Cox and Cooper 1988). Working long, intense work weeks (and many weekends) over a span of many years—a work pattern common among leaders—requires that an individual have a high level of physical, mental, and emotional vitality. A leader's visible display of energy enthusiastically communicates the vision and helps to increase employees' commitment to it.

Leaders are more likely than nonleaders to have a high level of energy and stamina, and even superior athletic ability (Bass 1990). They are generally lively, sometimes restless, and they can be characterized as "electric, vigorous, active, full of life" (Kouzes and Posner 1987, p. 122). Successful Sears executives have been found to "possess the physical vitality to maintain a steadily productive work pace" (Bentz 1967, pp. 117–18). Even at age seventy, Sam Walton, founder of Wal-Mart discount stores, still attended Wal-Mart's Saturday Morning Meeting, a whoop-it-up 7:30 A.M. sales pep rally for three hundred managers (Huey 1989).

Geographic expansion has made the need for energy even greater today than it was in the past, as more and more companies now expect their employees, at the executive and other levels, to spend more time on the road visiting the companies' other locations, customers, and suppliers (Peters 1987).

Tenacity is a motive that involves sustaining goal-directed energy across time when faced with obstacles. Leaders must be "tirelessly persistent" in their activities—especially in communicating their vision to employees (Bass 1990; Smith and Harrison 1986). When gaining commitment to the vision, leaders must adhere to the vision despite opposition and must follow through with what they implement.

Most changes in organizational programs take several months to get under way, and it can take many years before the benefits are seen. Leaders must have the drive to follow through and the persistence to ensure that changes are institutionalized into the organization. Considerable evidence indicates that effective leaders must possess tenacity—in abundance (Bass 1990; Smith and Harrison 1986).

Billionaire businessman H. Ross Perot, a U.S. Naval Academy alumnus, told the audience at the 1990 Forrestal Lecture Series at Annapolis that the academy had taught him to persevere in the face of adversity: "I think a lot of my business success comes from my inability to recognize that I had failed" (quoted in Munsey 1990, pp. C–1).

Effective leaders are more persistent than nonleaders in the face of obstacles, and they have the "capacity to work with distant objects in view" and have a "degree of strength of will or perseverance" (Bass 1990, p. 68).

A heroic illustration of perseverance in the face of obstacles is the tale of John Paul Jones, an eighteenth-century officer in the newly formed American Navy. On September 25, 1779, off the coast of England, Jones, captain of the *Bonhomme Richard,* engaged in battle with the British ship *Serapis.* In addition to being slow, unsuited to naval warfare, and lacking adequate cannons, Jones's ship was manned with an inexperienced hodge-podge crew from several different countries.

Jones appeared to have lost the battle after being bombarded with cannon fire by the *Serapis* and the explosion of two of his ship's old cannons. Jones suffered another setback when the *Alliance*—a supposed ally—fired upon his ship instead of upon the *Serapis.* The *Serapis* pulled alongside the *Bonhomme Richard,* and its captain demanded Jones's surrender. Jones's immortal reply, in the face of almost certain defeat, was, "I have not yet begun to fight."

Determined to sink the British ship, Jones spotted an open hatch on the *Serapis's* deck. He ordered a young sailor to climb into the rigging and toss grenades into the hatch, knowing the British had stored their ammunition there. After several failed attempts, a grenade disappeared into the hatchway, followed by a thunderous explosion. His ship engulfed in flames, the British captain surrendered what was left of the *Serapis* to Jones. Even though the entire battle had gone against him, Jones exhibited a determination not to give up, and it was this persistence that caused him to finally emerge victorious (De LaCroix 1962).

Thus, it is not simply the direction of a leader's action that counts but sticking with that direction. Being tenacious is the only way a leader can achieve a vision, and an effective leader must keep pushing himself and others toward the goal to be achieved (Bennis and Nanus 1985; Kouzes and Posner, 1987).

A number of well-known corporate leaders exhibit obvious tenacity. David Glass, CEO of Wal-Mart, says that owner Sam Walton "has an overriding something in him that causes him to improve every day. . . . As long as I have known him, he has never gotten to the point where he's comfortable with who he is or how we're doing" (quoted in Huey 1989, p. 58). Walt Disney has been described as expecting the best and not relenting until he got it (Smith and Harrison 1986). Ray Kroc, founder of McDonald's Corporation, has been described as a "dynamo who drove the company relentlessly" (Smith and Harrison, p. 27–5). Kroc posted this inspirational message on his wall:

> Nothing in the world can take the place of persistence.
> Talent will not; nothing is more common than unsuccessful
>   men with great talent.
> Genius will not; unrewarded genius is almost a proverb.
> Education will not; the world is full of educated derelicts.
> Persistence, determination alone are omnipotent. (quoted in
>   Bennis and Nanus 1985, p. 45)

Persistence, of course, must be applied intelligently. The dogged pursuit of an inappropriate strategy can bring an organization to ruin. So it is important to persist in the right things—but what are the right things? In most organizations operating in today's business climate, they include

- satisfying the customer,
- growth,
- cost control,
- innovation,
- fast response time, and
- quality.

Or as Tom Peters puts it (1987), a constant striving to improve just about everything.

Initiative is a motive that drives effective leaders to take a proactive rather than a reactive approach to their work (Bass 1990; Boyatzis 1982; Kouzes and Posner 1987). They make choices and do things that lead to productive change instead of just reacting to events or waiting for things to happen.

Superior managers and executive-level managers have been found to be more proactive than average-performing or lower-level managers. Proactivity among effective leaders is illustrated in the following three examples:

> I called the Chief, and he said he couldn't commit the resources, so I called the budget and finance people, who gave me a negative response. But then I called a guy in another work group who said he was willing to make a trade for the parts I needed. I got the parts and my group was able to complete the repairs.

> One of our competitors was making a short, half-inch component and probably making $30,000–$40,000 a year on it. I looked at our line: we have the same product and can probably make it better and cheaper. I told our marketing manager: "Let's go after that business." I made the decision that we would look at it as a marketplace rather than looking at it as individual customers wanting individual quantities. I said, here's a market that has 30,000 pieces of these things, and we don't give a damn where we get the orders. Let's just go out and get them. We decided we were going to charge a specific price and get the business. Right now we make $30,000–$40,000 on these things and our competitor makes zero.

> Delivery performance of one of our suppliers was down. So I went on a trip with the buyer as back-up support. We got there and met with two people who were incompetent. Their VPs had assured me that these two guys had the information. I was mad. I called the executive VP. It was gutsy because I went over the two VPs' heads and I was doing it rather than our buyer. I told him that we had a contractual agreement and that the performance of his company was horrible. I said that they were not paying attention to spares and that we didn't want to shut off the new contract but might have to if we didn't get the parts we needed. He gave me the party line and said he would remedy it. Well, the next day one of the VPs called me and was Mr. Humble. We got the parts and the delivery performance improved. (quoted in Boyatzis 1982, pp. 63, 73, 149)

Instead of sitting "idly by or [waiting] for fate to smile upon them," leaders need to "challenge the process" (Kouzes and Posner, p. 8). Effective leaders usually use a "hands on" approach and routinely show more initiative and enterprise than nonleaders (Bass 1990; Smith and Harrison 1986).

The evidence is clear that effective leaders are strongly driven— that is, highly achievement-oriented, ambitious, energetic, tenacious, and proactive. And these qualities are necessary if leaders are to effectively develop the knowledge, skills, and abilities (KSAs) needed to develop and implement a vision.

A high level of drive, however, is not without the potential for producing undesirable side-effects. This type of drive may result in a leader trying to accomplish everything alone and thereby failing to develop subordinates' commitment and sense of responsibility (McClelland and Burnham 1976). Effective leaders must not only be full of drive and ambition, they must be motivated to lead others.

Leadership Motivation

Effective leaders must *want* to lead. Leadership motivation involves the desire to influence others. It is often equated with the need for power. Persons with high leadership motivation think a lot about influencing other people, winning an argument, or attaining a position of greater authority. Individuals with strong leadership motivation prefer to be in a leadership role rather than in a subordinate role, and they exhibit a willingness to assume responsibility (Howard and Bray 1988; McClelland 1965; Yukl 1989). Studies confirm a strong desire to lead others to be characteristic of effective leaders (Boyatzis 1982; Burns 1978; House 1988; House, Woycke, and Fodor 1987; Miner 1978; Srivastva and Associates 1986).

Research on leadership traits at Sears describes successful Sears executives as those who have a "powerful competitive drive for a position of . . . authority . . . [and] the need to be recognized as men of influence" (Bentz 1967, p. 179).

Astronauts John Glenn and Frank Borman built political and business careers out of their early feats as space explorers, while other astronauts did not (Bass 1985). Possessing the same opportunities as the others, it was their personal makeup that caused Glenn and Borman to pursue their ambitions and take on leadership roles.

Successful leaders must be willing to exercise power over subordinates, to tell them what to do, and to make appropriate use of positive and negative sanctions. A person who is unable to exercise power will have difficulty performing in a leadership role.

Power can be viewed as a leader's currency: the primary means through which a leader gets things done in an organization (Bennis and Nanus 1985). A leader must have the desire to gain power in order to exercise influence over others. In one study, executive-level managers and those with higher performance levels ranked higher on "concern for impact" (considered to be similar to a need for power) than their lower-level managerial counterparts or those performing at a lower level of productivity (Boyatzis 1982).

In a twenty-year management study at AT&T, successful managers completed sentence fragments in the following manner:

"When I am in charge of others I *find my greatest satisfactions.*"

"The job I am best fit for *is one that requires leadership ability.*"

"I depend on *others to carry out my plans and directions.*"
(Howard and Bray 1988, pp. 146, 188)

By contrast, a manager who was not as successful completed the sentence fragment "Taking orders . . ." with the ending "*is easy for it removes the danger of a bad decision*" (Howard and Bray 1988, p. 189).

Power is most effectively utilized when it is viewed as an "expandable pie," not as a fixed sum. An effective leader does not see power as a static quantity that must be competed for. Rather, an effective leader sees power as something that can be created and distributed to followers without detracting from the leader's own power. Effective leaders actually give power to others as a means of increasing their own potency.

The need for power is desirable in a leader, yet the effectiveness of a leader depends on the roots of this need. The desire to influence others can stem from two different sources: a "personalized power motive" or a "socialized power motive" (Howell 1988; McClelland 1965).

PERSONALIZED POWER MOTIVE. A leader with a personalized power motive seeks power as an end in itself. Such individuals have little self-control and are often impulsive; they focus on collecting symbols of their own personal prestige. This type of power motive can be considered neurotic since acquiring power solely for the sake of dominating others must be based on profound self-doubt. The personalized power motive is concerned with domination of others and leads to dependent, submissive followers (Kouzes and Posner 1987).

SOCIALIZED POWER MOTIVE. By contrast, a leader with a socialized power motive uses power as a means to achieve a desired goal or vision. This motivation is more likely to result in effective leadership. Compared with those having personalized power motives, individuals with socialized power motives:

- are more emotionally mature;
- exercise power more for the benefit of the whole organization;
- are less likely to use power in a manipulative manner;
- are less defensive;
- are more willing to take advice from experts; and
- have longer-range perspectives. (Kouzes and Posner 1987)

Leaders with socialized power motives tend to use their power to build up their organization and make it successful, rather than to seek personal aggrandizement at the expense of others. They take into account their followers' needs, and their actions lead to empowered, independent followers.

The productive use of socialized power finds expression as the ability to develop networks and coalitions, gain cooperation from others, resolve conflicts in a constructive manner, and use role modeling to influence others.

The Core Traits

Our discussion of the core motives has focused on the underlying desires that impel a leader to action. In a sometimes subtle yet relevant distinction, *traits* are different from motives in that they are patterns of observable action—ways of behaving—or habitual ways of thinking. People are said to possess the trait of "charm," for example, when they characteristically act in a charming manner; they are said to be "pessimistic" if they habitually express negative thoughts.

Motives may underlie traits, but there is no one-to-one relationship between traits and motives. A given trait may reflect multiple motives, just as a given motive may underlie a number of traits.

This section explores core leadership traits—the observable acts and presumed thinking habits that are characteristic of effective leaders. (For the sake of clarity, the traits of energy, tenacity, and initiative were discussed in the section on motives because they are behavioral expressions of those motives.)

There is considerable evidence that effective leadership is characterized by the traits of honesty/integrity and self-confidence; there is less conclusive evidence regarding the role of the traits of creativity, flexibility, and charisma.

Honesty/Integrity

Honesty and integrity are undisputed virtues in all individuals (Rand 1961), including followers, but they have a special significance as traits for leaders. Studies show that without them, the whole enterprise of leadership is undermined (Bass 1990; Bennis and Nanus 1985; Peters 1987). *Integrity* is defined as a correspondence between word and deed (Bennis and Nanus 1985), and *honesty* refers to being truthful or nondeceitful. Together they constitute the foundation of a trusting relationship between a leader and his or her followers (Kouzes and Posner 1987).

In his comprehensive review of leadership, Bernard Bass (1990) found that among students, the leaders were rated as more dependable, trustworthy, and reliable in carrying out responsibilities than were their followers. Similarly, British researchers Charles Cox and Cary Cooper's (1988) "high flying" managers preferred to have an open style of management, in which they truthfully informed workers about happenings in the company. Researchers at the Center for Creative Leadership in Greensboro, North Carolina have found that managers who reached the top were more likely to espouse the following formula: "I will do exactly what I say I will do when I say I will do it. If I change my mind, I will tell you well in advance so you will not be harmed by my actions" (McCall and Lombardo 1983, p. 11).

Successful leaders are open with their followers, but they also use discretion and do not violate confidences or carelessly divulge potentially harmful information. Harvard's John Gabarro reports that one subordinate made the following remark about his new president: "He was so consistent in what he said and did, it was easy to trust him." Another subordinate remarked of an unsuccessful leader, "How can I rely on him if I can't count on him consistently?" (Gabarro 1987, p. 105).

In another study, fifteen hundred managers were asked "What values do you look for and admire in your superiors?" The study found that integrity (defined as being truthful, trustworthy, and having character and conviction) was the single most frequently mentioned characteristic. Leadership researchers James Kouzes and Barry Posner concluded:

> Honesty is absolutely essential to leadership. After all, if we are willing to follow someone, whether it be into battle or into the boardroom, we first want to assure ourselves that the person is worthy of our trust. We want to know that he or she is being truthful, ethical, and principled. We want to be fully confident in the integrity of our leaders. (Kouzes and Posner 1987, p. 18)

Many studies have found that effective leaders are consistently viewed as credible, having excellent reputations for trustworthiness (Bass 1990; Kotter 1988).

One subordinate's description of his boss exemplifies the meaning of *integrity:* "By integrity, I don't mean whether he'll rob a bank, or steal from the till. You don't work with people like that. It's whether you sense a person has some basic principles and is willing to stand by them" (Gabarro, p. 105).

But "credibility is at a premium these days," caution researchers Bennis and Nanus (1985, p. 11), especially since people are better informed, more cautious, and more wary of authority and power. They have found that leaders gain trust by being predictable, consistent, and persistent. To this, Gabarro (1987) adds the credibility-building trait of making competent decisions.

The astronomically successful businessman H. Ross Perot has said that applying the ethical code taught at the U.S. Naval Academy to one's personal life is one of the best things an individual can do. He urged the midshipmen, "Don't run your life by what's legal or illegal. Run your life based on what's right and wrong" (quoted in Munsey 1990, p. C-1).

A leader who is honest may even be able to overcome a lack of other skills, as illustrated by one subordinate's description of his superior: "I don't like a lot of the things he does, but he's basically honest. He's a genuine article and you'll forgive a lot of things because of that. That goes a long way in how much I trust him" (quoted in Gabarro 1987, p. 105).

Self-Confidence

That self-confidence is a necessary trait for successful leadership is undisputed. A person riddled with self-doubt when faced with challenges and responsibilities is not able to take the necessary actions or to command the respect of others. Leadership carries heavy challenges and responsibilities because

- a great deal of information must be gathered and processed;
- a constant series of problems must be solved and decisions made;
- followers have to be found and convinced to pursue specific courses of action;
- rewards and punishments must be administered;
- risks have to be taken in the face of uncertainty;
- setbacks have to be overcome; and
- competing interests have to be satisfied.

The essential nature of self-confidence, of having assurance in one's own ideas and abilities, has been recognized by many leadership researchers (Bennis and Nanus 1985; Burns 1978). Self-confidence plays an important role in decision-making and in gaining others' trust. A leader who is not sure of what decision to make, or who expresses a high degree of self-doubt, cannot develop the confidence among followers that is necessary to commit them to the vision.

Studies show conclusively that leaders typically have higher levels of self-confidence than nonleaders. Psychologist Bernard Bass, reviewing over forty studies, notes that "almost all authors reporting data on the relationship of self-confidence to leadership were uniform in the positive direction of their findings" (1990, p. 69). Concurring, Ann Howard and Douglas Bray (1988) found that AT&T managers' levels of self-esteem significantly predicted their degree of advancement twenty years later. Richard Boyatzis (1982) reveals that executive-level and superior managers are significantly higher in self-confidence—defined as decisiveness or presence—than lower-level managers or average or poor managers.

A study by Kouzes and Posner of leaders' "personal bests"—situations in which leaders accomplished something extraordinary—confirms that leaders possess a high degree of self-confidence.

> Each was excited by and willing to accept the challenges they faced, either by circumstance or by choice. Without exception or hesitation, these people expressed confidence that they could work well with others and assemble a team to address whatever problems might lie ahead. The high expectations that leaders have of others are based in large part of their expectations of themselves. (1987, p. 243)

Not only is a leader's self-confidence important; the leader must take steps to ensure that others perceive that self-confidence. Leaders often take actions to project their self-confidence, as well as to arouse their followers' own self-confidence (Bass 1985).

Self-confident leaders are also more likely to be assertive and decisive (Bass 1990; Cox and Cooper 1988), which helps them gain others' confidence in their decisions. This is crucial for the effective implementation of a decision.

Even when a decision a leader makes turns out to be a poor one, the self-confident leader can use it as a learning opportunity by admitting the mistake and can often build trust in the process. The firm Manor Care, for example, lost more than $21 million in 1988 when it was caught holding a large chunk of Beverly Enterprises' stock, which later slumped in value. Chairman and CEO Stewart Bainum, Jr., stated, "I take full and complete responsibility for making the acquisition" (quoted in Girard 1989, p. 70). Manor Care appears to be making a comeback now. Considered to be the "best managed company in the [nursing home] industry" (p. 72), Manor Care's stock has rebounded.

On the other hand, studies have found that less successful, "derailed" managers were often more defensive about their failures and tried to cover up their mistakes rather than admit them (McCall and Lombardo 1983).

A correlate and consequence of self-confidence is *emotional stability* and composure under stress. Although effective leaders get appropriately excited on occasions—such as when delivering an emotionally charged pep talk—they generally do not become angry or enraged. Rather, they exhibit an even temper (Bass 1990; Kotter 1982) that lets them remain composed—even upon hearing bad news.

University of Maryland researchers Ken G. Smith and Kline Harrison (1986) found that the leaders they studied were not as calm and tolerant as other literature had often suggested, but the consensus nonetheless is that most leaders are tolerant of unforeseeable employee mistakes. At PepsiCo, for example, an employee who makes a mistake is "safe . . . as long as it's a calculated risk" (Dumaine 1989, p. 86). This is true in other corporate settings that have been studied (Posner and Solomon 1988), as long as it is believed that the error was not a careless one and that employees did their homework yet had somehow misjudged the situation.

Emotional stability is especially important when a leader is resolving interpersonal conflicts or representing the organization. A top executive whose emotions impulsively erupt does not elicit the degree of trust and teamwork that is elicited by the executive who retains emotional control. Describing this negative trait in his superior, one employee stated, "He's impulsive and I'm never sure when he'll change signals on me" (quoted in Gabarro 1987, p. 105).

Researchers at the Center for Creative Leadership, attempting to identify traits associated with eventual success or failure of top executives (McCall and Lombardo 1983), have found that leaders are more likely to derail if they lack emotional stability and composure. The derailed leaders are those who are less able to handle pressure and who are more prone to moodiness, angry outbursts, and inconsistent behavior, which undermines their interpersonal relationships with subordinates, peers, and superiors. By contrast, the researchers found, the successful leaders are calm, confident, and predictable during crises.

Howard and Bray (1988) found that high adjustment (*adjustment* is somewhat nebulously defined in their study but appears to resemble positive mental health) in AT&T managers was related to their career advancement twenty years later. The more adjusted managers had advanced further in their careers. Overall, poor adjustment was reflected in managers' lower levels of performance. In their study, tolerance of uncertainty had low but significant correlations with career advancement.

How a leader deals with uncertainty and stress has a bearing on his or her effectiveness. Psychologically hardy, self-confident individuals

- consider stressful events interesting;
- believe that they can influence the outcome of such events; and
- see them as opportunities for development. (Maddi and Kobasa 1984)

Leaders demonstrate grace under pressure and inspire those around them to stay calm and act intelligently (Labich 1988).

Originality/Creativity

There are several reasons to hesitate to include originality and creativity among *essential* leadership traits. The limited research that has been done on creativity has shown positive results (Bass 1990), but creativity is rarely mentioned as a necessary trait in any of the qualitative studies of leaders.

It may be that creativity becomes helpful for effective leadership only in certain situations, such as when entrepreneurs are faced with developing a new product or service or with building a company from the ground up. Creativity may or may not be closely related to intelligence, discussed in the next section.

Expanding the concept of creativity to include resourcefulness, Bass's review of several studies (1990) finds that leaders are more resourceful than nonleaders. Also, effective managers exhibit more of the competency called conceptualization than do ineffective managers (Boyatzis 1982). Conceptualization, in Boyatzis's study, includes the ability to develop creative solutions and new insights into problems. Howard and Bray's (1988) longitudinal study of AT&T managers includes creativity as a subscale of administrative ability; their results indicate that administrative skills are positively related to managerial advancement.

But a leader can still be effective with good ideas that are borrowed rather than original. Tom Watson of IBM, for example, used many of the sales strategies he learned while at National Cash Register to make IBM into a leading sales organization (Smith and Harrison 1986). Soichiro Honda, founder of Honda Motor Company, did not invent the internal combustion engine, but he helped to improve and perfect it.

A concept that is related to originality is imagination. Professor Abraham Zaleznik, who defines *imagination* as the ability to visualize what might be, states that in business (as opposed to the arts), imagination is "largely imitative and applied . . . it searches for solutions based on experience and analogy" (1989, p. 218). Zaleznik, implying that imagination *is* a crucial trait for effective leadership, details how those without it sometimes try to compensate: "to overcome a lack of imagination, authority figures may try to apply charm, seduction, and even deviousness—tactics that in the end diminish their authority" (1989, p. 215).

Imagination is especially important for developing a vision, but it is not clear whether it is *required* in order to develop an effective vision. Effective leaders may be able to overcome their own personal lack of imagination or originality by inspiring others to suggest creative ideas. Some leaders, for example, are very good at having their top management team jointly develop their company's vision instead of developing that vision alone (Tichy and Devanna 1986), so leaders may need only to nurture creativity in others—rather than possess it themselves—to be effective.

Flexibility/Adaptability

An effective leader must be flexible enough to meet the challenges of the vigorous and rapid changes that are taking place in corporate America and the turbulent world economy (Bass 1990; Boyatzis 1982). Tom Peters advises leaders, "These wild and woolly times call for a new species of competitor—fast, agile, thriving on change" (1989, p. 92). These changes have occurred on a number of levels.

- Sophisticated technological advances have made it possible to speed up production.
- New services are constantly being offered and developed to attract and retain customers.

• Customers demand the latest products in the least amount of time.

Speed and *rapid change* were the catchwords of the eighties and are also characteristics of the nineties. To handle and foster change, leaders must be flexible. Note that in this context, *flexibility* refers to the ability to adapt to changing circumstances; it does not refer to being indecisive.

Flexibility (defined as adjusting to situations) is associated with leadership capacity in a number of the studies reviewed by Bass (1990). Using the term *versatility,* Hickman and Silva (1984) discuss its importance as the capacity to participate in the change process and to perform more creatively and powerfully. Without flexibility, leaders may become set in their ways, isolated with fixed ideas, and unable to adapt to changes in the environment and organization.

Flexibility and adaptability can also be applied to ideas and visions. A number of "idea borrowers" successfully adapted ideas to meet their companies' needs, such as IBM's Watson, mentioned earlier, who used many of the concepts he had learned at NCR to make IBM a leader in its field. Similarly, Ray Kroc borrowed and expanded the McDonald brothers' idea for fast-food restaurants. Charles Revson (of Revlon) adapted the General Motors idea of separate automotive product lines to the formation of separate cosmetic lines (Smith and Harrison 1986).

In addition to being flexible in adapting new ideas to their organizations, leaders are able to change their own leadership emphasis from task-oriented to people-oriented, as the situation demands (Smith and Harrison 1986).

Although flexibility may at first seem to contradict tenacity, they are not opposing traits. Tenacity involves continuing to work to accomplish a worthwhile task even when one is presented with obstacles and difficulties. Flexibility is the ability to recognize when there is a need to change one's way of addressing the obstacles and difficulties.

Including flexibility as an essential leadership trait requires some disclaimers. Although there is evidence that effective leaders exhibit flexibility, it is not certain that those who research leaders' flexibility use the same definition or employ the same measures of flexibilty. For example, should *flexibility* be taken to mean

- changing one's leadership style as the situation demands?
- being open to new knowledge and new ideas?
- frequently changing organizational strategies?
- giving in to customer demands?
- changing organizational policies and procedures?

Unfortunately, there is no way to tell from the studies conducted to date what definition of *flexibility* they used. Also, flexibility, like creativity, is rarely mentioned in the qualitative studies.

Charisma

Charisma is a widely studied characteristic of leaders (Bass 1985; Conger 1988; House, Woycke, and Fodor 1987), but there is some confusion as to what it actually means. Kouzes and Posner report that Friedman and his colleagues "found that those who were perceived to be charismatic were simply more animated than others. They smiled more, spoke faster, pronounced words more clearly, and moved their heads and bodies more often. They were also more likely to touch others during greetings. What we call charisma can better be understood as human expressiveness" (1987, pp. 123–24). Charisma is most visible as a power to arouse emotions in others and as such is probably measurable.

Charisma exerts its greatest impact during communication, especially when a leader is giving an inspirational speech to motivate subordinates (Bass 1990; Smith and Harrison 1986). But the vision of a leader who relies primarily on charisma is not institutionalized throughout the organization, and the vision usually fades when the leader dies or leaves (Bass 1985).

Charisma, like leadership, exists only in a relationship between leaders and followers; it cannot exist independently of followers. Thus, the same individual may be felt to have charisma by one group of followers but not by another. For example, during his first term as president, many Americans considered Ronald Reagan to be highly charismatic, but many others did not.

Charisma helps to reduce "resistance to attitude change in followers and . . . arousing emotional responses toward the leader and a sense of excitement and adventure" (Bass 1985, p. 56). Martin Luther King, Jr., electrified his followers with his "I Have a Dream" speech, in which he said that one day Black Americans would be "free at last."

Despite group pressure on followers to perform at a low level, followers of charismatic leaders show higher performance than followers of "structuring" (task-oriented) or "considerate" (relationship-oriented) leaders (Howell and Frost 1989). Supporting these findings, Smith (cited in Bass 1985) finds that subordinates under charismatic leaders often work longer work weeks and are more confident and trusting than subordinates under noncharismatic leaders.

When charisma is present in a leader, it has positive effects on the followers' motivation, self-esteem, and attitudes. When followers perceive a leader as charismatic, charisma becomes a self-fulfilling prophecy, and the leader is able to produce more and more charismatic effects. The chain reaction becomes one in which perceived charisma influences the leader's behavior, which then affects performance (House, Woycke, and Fodor 1987).

Other specific behaviors exhibited by charismatic leaders, according to House, Woycke, and Fodor (1987) are that they

- articulate a transcendent goal (a vision);
- serve as role models;
- build their own image;
- show strong confidence in followers;
- communicate high follower-performance expectations;
- arouse needs for achievement, power, and/or affiliation; and
- have a developmental attitude toward subordinates.

United States presidents Thomas Jefferson, Andrew Jackson, Abraham Lincoln, Theodore Roosevelt, Franklin D. Roosevelt, and John F. Kennedy are identified by House, Woycke, and Fodor (1987) as charismatic leaders. Other presidents are categorized as either neutral or noncharismatic. Their results show that while only a relatively small percentage of neutral or noncharismatic presidents were either re-elected or assassinated, all of the charismatic leaders fell into one or both of those groupings, suggesting that they aroused strong feelings in others. House and colleagues also found that charisma accounts for almost half of the factors contributing to a leader's effectiveness, as rated from encyclopedia articles. (It should be noted that this measure is problematic in that it depends on the political views of those writing the encyclopedia entries.)

Despite its alleged benefits, charisma may not be an essential trait for leaders. George Washington, for example, did not exhibit charismatic attributes, but he was generally considered a great political and military leader. It may be the case that "leaders can be successful in many other ways without the attributes of charisma," such as successfully resolving conflicts and providing contingent rewards for compliance (Bass 1985, p. 49).

Bennis and Nanus conclude that although some leaders are charismatic, most are not. Leaders such as John F. Kennedy and Winston Churchill are considered charismatic, but most leaders are all "too human" (1985, p. 223). The leaders that Bennis and Nanus studied were "short and tall, articulate and inarticulate, dressed for success and dressed for failure, and there was virtually nothing in terms of physical appearance, personality, or style that set them apart from their followers." This led the researchers to speculate that instead of charisma resulting in effective leadership, the reverse may be true; those who are effective leaders are granted charisma (respect and awe) by their followers as a *result* of their success.

Summary

The evidence is clear that in crucial respects, leaders are different from other people. Successful leaders are strongly driven, have a strong desire to lead and exercise power, exhibit honesty and integrity, and are highly self-confident. These four core characteristics are so fundamental that it is doubtful whether a severe deficiency in one of them can be compensated for by the presence of others. Bonus traits, often helpful but perhaps not essential, are creativity, flexibility, and charisma.

Possessing even the four key characteristics alone is not enough. Effective leaders must also possess or acquire important knowledge, skills, and abilities, and these aspects of leadership are covered in the next chapter.

3

Knowledge, Skills, and Ability

Although possessing the key motives and traits does not by itself make an effective leader, those motives and traits can help an individual acquire the knowledge and skills necessary to formulate a leader's vision and implement it. Ability, too, especially cognitive ability, plays a vital role in leadership.

Knowledge

Technological expertise often facilitates a leader's ability to lead an organization. A review of eleven studies conducted between 1904 and 1947 (Bass 1981) found that all concluded that specialized knowledge is a key contributor to leadership status.

A contemporary corporate example of such expertise is George N. Hatsopolous, the founder, chairman and president of Thermo Electron Corporation. In the years preceding the 1973 OPEC (Organization of Petroleum Exporting Countries) boycott, Hatsopolous had the knowledge of the impending need for energy-efficient appliances as well as the technological knowledge of thermodynamics to create more efficient gas furnaces and have them in production by the time demand arose (Posner and Solomon 1988).

Citing more recent examples of technological expertise, Labich writes, "What August Busch of Anheuser-Busch doesn't know about beer probably isn't worth knowing" (1988, p. 62). And Jack Welch, the chairman of General Electric, who earned a Ph.D. in

---

Chapter 3 was written mainly by Kathryn Niles.

engineering, is described as being "comfortable with technology" (Sherman 1989, p. 42). Not only do these leaders have technological knowledge, their knowledge is visible to those around them.

In his study of leadership, Kenneth Labich (1988) concludes that being an expert (which involves knowing about the company's product) is crucial to effective leadership and can be gained through experience.

In addition to aiding the technological advancement of their companies, having such expertise also allows leaders to better understand the concerns of their subordinates regarding technical issues. This understanding in turn facilitates the interpersonal aspects of leadership that will be discussed later.

Understandably, while having technological expertise *alone* is beneficial or even necessary in some leadership positions, it is not sufficient to make someone an effective leader. Leaders may rise through the ranks due to their technical knowledge of a special segment or area, but once they are at the top, they must be knowledgeable in a number of other areas to succeed. One study (Yukl 1989) finds that managers who fail to perform successfully tend to be specialists whose technical expertise has been their *sole* path to success at lower levels of management. At higher levels, this becomes a weakness if it leads to arrogance based on a narrow vision.

Knowledge of the organization and industry often has greater importance than formal education (Gabarro 1987; Kotter 1988). Only 40 percent of the effective leaders studied by Bennis and Nanus (1985) had business degrees. According to Kotter (1982), leaders must possess extensive information about the business and their organization in order to achieve success. His study of fifteen successful general managers found that they had spent 81 percent of their careers in their current companies and 91 percent of their careers in their current industries (broadly defined), developing detailed knowledge based on their experience. In Gabarro's (1987) study of seventeen top managers, a lack of industry-specific experience was a characteristic of three out of four failed leadership successions but characterized less than half of the successful ones.

None of the leaders studied by Smith and Harrison—including Ray Kroc (McDonald's), Walt Disney (Disney), and Tom Watson (IBM)—had had extensive formal training in business. But "each demonstrated specific, in-depth knowledge and expertise in the hows and whys of his organization's success" (Smith and Harrison 1986, pp. 27–29). This expertise allowed them to make well-informed decisions and have a better understanding of the implications of those decisions.

Knowledge of the industry and organization allows a leader to fall back on past experience to make rational decisions quickly (Fiedler and Garcia 1987). In this vein, many companies, such as PepsiCo, are implementing job-rotation programs to broaden their employees' knowledge of the organization (Dumaine 1989; Peters 1987).

A leader's experience is the basis for his or her knowledge that can intellectually stimulate and broaden subordinates' understanding of organizational issues. Bass suggests that intellectual stimulation does not refer to scholarly knowledge but to "the arousal and change in followers of problem awareness and problem solving, of thought and imagination, and of belief and values" (1985, p. 99). This is a process of motivating and guiding subordinates.

Skills

Interpersonal Skills

Having *people skills* is important because leadership is a relationship that depends on the interaction between a leader and followers for its very existence. A leader's interpersonal skills are vitally important in the process of inspiring others toward implementing the vision. Insensitivity to others has been found to be a primary reason that formerly successful executives become derailed, in research conducted by the Center for Creative Leadership (McCall and Lombardo 1983). By contrast, successful leaders generally have very strong interpersonal skills, deal with other people well, and are diplomatic and tactful (Bennis and Nanus 1985; Cox and Cooper 1988; Gabarro 1987; Howard and Bray 1988; McCall and Lombardo 1983; Yukl 1989).

One interpersonal factor affecting subordinates' satisfaction and leadership effectiveness is the *consideration* the leader shows. The Ohio State University and University of Michigan leadership studies (Yukl 1989) define consideration as being displayed through the degree to which leaders

- act in a friendly and supportive manner;
- show concern for subordinates;
- look out for subordinates' welfare;
- show trust and confidence;
- try to understand subordinates' problems;
- help develop subordinates and further their careers; and
- keep subordinates informed.

Certain other interpersonal skills are also critical in leaders' efforts to communicate their visions, induce others to join their networks, and obtain the support of group members. These skills include:

- listening,
- oral communication,
- network-building,
- conflict management, and
- assessing self and others. (Bray, Campbell, and Grant 1974; Dunnette 1971; Kotter 1982; Yukl 1989)

Listening skills help a leader build trust through both formal and informal communication with others. Because listening skills allow a leader to use the ideas and experiences of others as an information resource, they are also a primary means of gathering information to develop the vision, to motivate followers, and to develop suitable strategies (Bennis and Nanus 1985; Kouzes and Posner 1987). Listening also serves as a mechanism for receiving feedback from subordinates regarding how the leader is viewed.

Peters recommends that leaders at all levels in an organization make a conscious effort to listen to their employees and to integrate and act on the information they receive. He notes, "If talking and giving orders was the administrative model of the last fifty years, listening (to lots of people near the action) is the model of the 1980s and beyond" (1987, p. 524).

Listening is a particularly essential interpersonal skill for a new manager. New managers learn about their organizations this way, and subordinates appreciate the interest shown in them as individuals. One new manager used listening skills to the benefit of both himself and his subordinates, as described by one of his subordinates:

The first thing he did when he came was to interview the top two levels in the organization—just talking to people. Then he came back. In my case, I opened up about what the problems were and he was a real good listener. He spent a lot of time with me. . . . The time wasn't important to him—he was willing to listen. I think this is why most people felt comfortable opening up to him. . . . He also kept coming back later and checking back. (quoted in Gabarro 1987, p. 117)

"Active listening" is widely used by effective leaders. Specifically, active listening involves restating and/or interpreting what others have said so that they are assured that their message is being received (Gordon 1977). A simple example is the following brief exchange:

Message sender: What's the use of trying to change things around here?
Listener: You're feeling very discouraged.

The message sender may then choose to confirm or correct the listener's interpretation but is assured that the listener is indeed listening.

Gordon (1977) suggests that active listening can be used to

- calm heated discussions so that underlying issues can be uncovered;
- determine and address personal concerns of subordinates; and
- teach subordinates more effectively by creating a more empathic and accepting environment.

Oral communication skills correlated significantly with managerial success at AT&T (Howard and Bray 1988). Successful leaders are generally found to

- speak fluently (Boyatzis 1982; Yulk 1989),
- have a pleasing voice (Bass 1981),
- have superior debating skills (Bass 1985), and
- show confidence by their tone of voice (Stogdill 1974). (This is even true of young children who are leaders of their peers.)

To emphasize the importance of oral communication skills for effective leadership, Bennis and Nanus say, "The management of meaning, mastery of communication, is inseparable from effective leadership" (1985, p. 33).

A leader's ability to communicate a message may be as important as the message itself. Ronald Reagan, for example, had the ability to communicate abstract topics using concrete examples that the public could understand. On the other hand, even though Jimmy Carter is considered one of the best-informed of recent presidents, he was an unimpressive communicator (Bennis and Nanus 1985). Reagan was re-elected; Carter was not.

One of the interpersonal skills that is characteristic of many leaders is *expressiveness* in communicating with others. Expressiveness is sometimes called charisma (see Chapter 2), but it need not involve the strong emotional appeal that charisma connotes. Expressiveness involves presenting information in a way that engages and motivates followers by addressing their interests and needs, not just their emotions.

Effective communication is not limited to verbal communication skills. Bill Moog, successful manufacturer of aircraft engine parts at Moog, Inc., is described by Bennis and Nanus as being somewhat taciturn. But when Moog was asked how he communicates, he replied,

> Seems to me that when I feel strongly about something, people know it. I'm not sure how or why. I do draw pictures from time to time and send those out or else I build a model. When we decentralized a couple of years ago, I sent around a mock-up of the way I wanted our organization to look. Drew it on graph paper . . . people seemed to get it. (quoted in Bennis and Nanus 1985, p. 35)

Indeed, effective leaders use a variety of communication techniques—such as metaphors, slogans, and models—to clarify their vision.

Network-building is another key interpersonal skill of effective leaders. In managerial transitions, the determinant of success is often the quality of the manager's working relationships with three factions: subordinates, peers, and supervisors. Gabarro (1987) finds that those leaders who are successful have interactive relationships within the organization through group meetings and the use of task forces, in which more interaction takes place. In Gabarro's study, at the end of twelve months,

> Three of four managers in failed successions had poor working relationships with two or more of their key subordinates. . . . Three out of four also had poor relationships with two or more peers, and all had poor relationships with their superiors. . . . In contrast, only three of the thirteen new managers in the successful transitions had a poor relationship with their boss at the end of that period and none had poor relationships with as many as two of their direct reports. (1987, p. 57)

This conclusion reinforces the importance of building networks to the success of a leader.

Network-building is important outside the organization as well as within. External network-building provides top managers with extensive knowledge about what is happening in the industry and about who has expertise in every aspect of the business and the business environment (Kotter 1982).

The skill of networking has been conceptualized as developing a system of trade routes to gain the information and power needed to get things done (Kaplan and Mazique 1983). Networking relationships are based on a principle of reciprocity between leaders in lateral positions. Networking alliances may begin through common contacts or personal history, but they are sustained because each of those involved has the power to accomplish things that the other needs now or anticipates needing in the future. The advantages gained in networking exchanges can include

- exclusive or expert information,
- connections to other parties,
- influence in building support, and
- input for making decisions.

Conflict-management skills are often required of those in positions of leadership when they are called upon to resolve dissension between subordinates or among various factions in the organization. (The trait of emotional stability also comes into play in such instances.)

The necessity of having conflict-resolution skills is described by

David L. Birch, president of Cognetics and the director of MIT's Program on Corporate Change and Job Creation this way:

> The one thing I hadn't banked on at all is the extent to which a company becomes a community. I thought people would come to work, do their jobs, and go home. . . . But I hadn't thought about how much time I'd have to spend adjudicating the frictions in that system so it remains a positive force—balancing all interests. . . . One way or another, I spend probably a quarter of my time on this. ("Coming of Age" 1989, p. 39)

Another important people skill for leaders is *assessment,* both of their own skills and of those of others. Assessment facilitates maximum utilization of employees' skills and permits successful team-building (Bennis and Nanus 1985; Kouzes and Posner 1987).

Assessment of others is needed to place the right people in the right positions and to know what those individuals find challenging. To aid in proper placement, a leader must discover

- individuals' expectations regarding the organization,
- what individuals want to gain from their work experiences, and
- individuals' needs, values, strengths, and weaknesses.

Beverly Ann Scott, organization-development manager at McKesson, tells leaders that to enlist people in their visions, they must "know [their] followers and speak their language" (quoted in Kouzes and Posner 1987, p. 10).

Effective leaders are sensitive to their followers. "Most leaders fail or succeed on their ability to know and understand the people they work with. You get the results of your efforts through other people, so you have to be very sensitive to each person and to their particular needs," states Russ Barnett, managing director of Metro-Brick in Western Australia (quoted in Kouzes and Posner 1987, p. 167).

Effective leaders also know their own strengths and weaknesses. This is especially important when building the top management team, because a leader's weaknesses must be compensated for by complementary strengths in others (Hambrick 1987). The leader can then delegate tasks appropriately to competent subordinates. This builds trust between the subordinates and the leader, increases the subordinates' autonomy, and further develops the subordinates' skills.

Management Skills and Competencies

Administrative skills are vital in carrying out the traditional management functions that facilitate the day-to-day activities of an organization. These skills include problem-solving, decision-making, goal-setting, and planning (Boyatzis 1982; Howard and Bray 1988; Kotter 1982). When working to implement a vision, and to help in the direct translations of the vision into the organization's daily activities, a leader often assumes a more administrative or managerial role. Administrative skills are not the same as management style. Rather, they are the competencies that allow leaders to perform tasks in whatever style they choose.

The classic Michigan studies (summarized in Yukl 1989) examined the role of effective and ineffective leaders in attaining group productivity. Effective leaders were found to concentrate on task-oriented behaviors, such as planning and scheduling work, coordinating subordinate activities, and providing technical assistance and resources. They also tended to guide subordinates in setting high but realistic performance goals. Administrative ability (based on in-basket measures of organizing, planning, and decision-making) was found by Howard and Bray (1988) to be predictive of managerial success, and Cox and Cooper (1988) report that successful managing directors in the United Kingdom consistently exhibit skills in problem-solving and decision-making.

Problem-solving and decision-making skills are closely related to the cognitive activity of conceptualizing. They depend on a leader's ability to grasp a situation and determine an appropriate course of action. Having such insight allows a leader to address the "heart of the problem" (Hickman and Silva 1984). In this manner, the impact of future problems can be lessened or even avoided altogether.

Leaders who are experienced in a company or industry often use intuition (or subconscious knowledge based on past experience) to solve familiar problems. More intractable problems may require more formalized techniques, such as Kepner and Tregoe's (1981) problem-analysis method.

The effective-management skill cluster developed by Boyatzis

(1982) incorporates skills in problem-solving, including logical thought and conceptualization. The effective use of this skill is described by one manager this way:

> I get a particular satisfaction out of acing out the competition by using strategies. . . . One particular strategy that comes to mind is when we were bidding 183 pieces of component parts. We had been in competition with SYSCOMP. By taking a look at their bidding history and their track record, at the eleventh hour before the bid goes in, I honed in on the price I thought they would bid. It turns out that by doing that we got the order because we were lower by $1.75 per piece. I did it by going back through history of bids of SYSCOMP against us over the past three years. I put myself in their shoes and asked what would they do in this situation. I concluded that they would drop their initial price by 6 percent at the end, which would have been $3 per piece. Fortunately, we were just about dead on. (quoted in Boyatzis 1982, pp. 112–13)

Ackoff (1978) points out that solving unstructured problems requires leaders and managers to constantly check their assumptions about factors such as

- what the problem really is;
- what people want as an outcome;
- what the facts are;
- what is a cause (as opposed to a correlation);
- what the actual scope of the problem is; and
- what the solution will look like.

Creative problem-solving requires thinking outside the scope of one's normal assumptions (that is, thinking "outside the square").

Effective decision-makers tend to use procedures that differ from those of ineffective decision-makers. Better decisions are made, assert Wheeler and Janis (1980), when leaders and managers (not to mention followers)

- accept the challenge (rather than deny the problem);
- generate many alternate solutions for consideration;
- evaluate each alternative with respect to the goals they want to achieve;
- commit themselves to a specific course of action after due consideration of the alternatives; and

- deal constructively with setbacks, such as by implementing a contingency plan or diagnosing the reasons for failure.

Vroom and Jago (1988) find that effective leaders and managers are more likely than less effective ones to use subordinate participation appropriately when they are making decisions. The effectiveness of subordinate participation is affected by

- subordinates' having (or being given) knowledge relevant to the issue in question;
- subordinates' sharing the values of the organization;
- having sufficient time to involve subordinates appropriately; and
- whether subordinates are likely to reject the solution unless they are consulted.

The art of skillfully involving subordinates is, like most management skills, obtainable through training.

Goal-setting is another administrative or management skill that is typically seen in effective leaders (Gardner 1986–88; Kotter 1982; Locke and Latham 1984, 1990). In his study of competent managers, Boyatzis (1982) included the skill of setting goals that are "challenging but realistic" as characteristic of managers who have an efficiency orientation—a concern to do things better. Having the skill to determine group and individual goals and to guide their achievement (discussed in greater detail in Chapter 5) is crucial to the implementation of a vision.

Planning is a necessary concomitant of goal-setting; it identifies the means by which goals are to be achieved. Entrepreneur Steve Bostic, who increased the sales of his American Photo Group 52,000 percent in five years and then sold it to Kodak for $45 million, does not believe that business success requires special talent for charisma. Rather, he believes that it requires "a passion for planning" (quoted in Gendron and Burlingham 1989, p. 47).

According to leading strategic-management thinkers, skillful planning involves

- a future orientation,
- extensive interaction and communication between organization members,

- a systematic and comprehensive analysis of the organization's strengths and weaknesses,
- an analysis of the opportunities and threats that the organization faces,
- a clear definition of the rules and functions all members and departments are to play, and
- the appropriate allocation of resources to support the plans. (Lorange and Vancil 1977; Steiner 1969)

Ability

Cognitive ability (intelligence) is an asset to leaders because leaders must gather, integrate, and interpret enormous amounts of information. Even if computers are utilized, as is prevalent today, information-processing still demands intense cognitive ability. Demands for cognitive ability have increased with the rapid pace of technological change. Leaders need a high level of such ability to formulate suitable strategies, solve problems, and make correct decisions.

Leaders are often characterized as intelligent and conceptually skilled people (Boyatzis 1982; Yukl 1989), but not necessarily as brilliant (Bass 1981, 1985; Howard and Bray 1988). Kotter identifies the need for a leader to have a "keen mind" (1982, 1988), which means possessing

- strong analytical ability,
- good judgment,
- the capacity to think strategically,
- the ability to think multidimensionally, and
- "above-average intelligence," rather than genius.

The correlation between individuals' intelligence and whether they are perceived as leaders has been found by Lord, De Vader, and Alliger (1986) to be statistically significant. They conclude that "intelligence is a key characteristic in predicting leadership perceptions."

Intelligence (measured through paper-and-pencil tests of verbal and quantitative ability, logical reasoning, and current affairs) has been found to be the cognitive ability that best predicted managerial success twenty years after entry into AT&T (Howard and Bray 1988). More specifically, Boyatzis (1982) finds that effective managers display greater ability to reason both inductively and deductively than do ineffective managers.

Intelligence appears to be a trait that followers look for in a leader. If someone is going to lead them, followers want that person to be more capable at least in *some* respects than they are. Therefore, the followers' perception of cognitive ability in a leader provides the leader with a source of legitimate and expert authority in the leader-follower relationship.

Cognitive ability is only partly determined by heredity. This leaves open the possibility that it can be developed further through effort and persistence. Although a general potential for intellectual ability may be inherited, it is what one *does* with that potential that determines one's ultimate level of intelligence and achievement.

Summary

The importance of a leader's knowledge, skills, and ability for his or her effectiveness is both intuitively and empirically clear. These include technological expertise, knowledge of the industry, people skills, administrative skills, and cognitive ability. It is through these personal competencies that leaders are able to develop and implement their visions.

4

Vision

It is through creation of a vision that leaders integrate and guide the efforts of all the members of their organizations. Without a vision, the motives, traits, knowledge, skills, and abilities already discussed will not ultimately matter. Some of the activities used to implement a vision (covered in Chapter 5) also are used, on a smaller scale, in the process of formulating and promoting the vision.

Defining *Vision*

Whether they call it vision, overarching goal, mission, agenda, central purpose, or another comparable term, effective leaders recognize its importance. Everything a leader does must be in accord with and in support of the vision. The key function of a leader is to establish a vision for the organization and to communicate it in a compelling way to the followers.

Exactly what is vision? Kouzes and Posner define *vision* as "an ideal and unique image of the future" (1987, p. 85). Hickman and Silva describe it as "a mental journey from the known to the unknown, creating the future from a montage of current facts, hopes, dreams, dangers, and opportunities" (1984, p. 151). But Bennis and Nanus seem to best capture the meaning of *vision* with these words:

> To choose a direction, a leader must first have developed a mental image of a possible and desirable future state of the organization.

Chapter 4 was written mainly by Jill Wheeler.

This image, which we call vision, may be as vague as a dream or as precise as a goal or a mission statement. The critical point is that a vision articulates a view of a realistic, credible, attractive future for the organization, a condition that is better in some important ways than what now exists. A vision is a target that beckons. (1985, p. 89)

A leader's vision may be complex and elaborate. It may contain many details, express many of the leader's values and incorporate various ideas for company strategies. It may include numerous ideas about what types of products will be made, what types of employees will be hired, and how customers will be treated. It may be fuzzy and undeveloped in places, and clear and distinct in others.

Organizational leaders express their convictions about vision in various ways:

> To manage is to lead, and to lead others requires that one
>   enlist the emotions of others to share a vision as their own.
> —Henry M. Boettinger, retired director of corporate planning,
>   AT&T (quoted in Kouzes and Posner 1987, p. 79)
> The leader's job is to create a vision.
> —Robert L. Swiggett, Chairperson, Kollmorgen Corporation
>   (quoted in Kouzes and Posner 1987, p. 81)

Joe Nevin, management information systems director at Apple Computer, describes leaders as "painters of the vision and architects of the journey" (quoted in Kouzes and Posner 1987, p. 83). Similarly, Bennis and Nanus view formulating the vision as the "core responsibility" of the leader and contend that the development and organizational integration of the vision are fundamental components of leadership (1985, p. 141).

Max DePree, CEO of the world-famous and highly profitable Herman Miller company (which designs and manufactures office furniture), argues that it is vision that gives a company momentum. He defines *momentum* as "the feeling among a group of people that their lives and work are intertwined and moving toward recognizable and legitimate goals" (DePree 1989, p. 14).

Vision Statements

The problem with complex visions is that they cannot be communicated succinctly to subordinates and customers. Consider, for example, Levi Strauss & Co.'s somewhat wordy declaration in what it terms its "aspirations statement":

> We all want a company that people are proud of and committed to, where all employees have an opportunity to contribute, learn, grow, and advance based on merit, not politics or background. We want our people to feel respected, treated fairly, listened to, and involved. Above all, we want satisfaction from accomplishment and friendships, balanced personal and professional lives, and to have fun in our endeavor.
>
> When we describe the kind of Levi Strauss & Co. we want in the future, what we are talking about is building on the foundation we have inherited: affirming the best of our company's traditions, closing gaps that may exist between principles and practices, and updating some of our values to reflect contemporary circumstances. (quoted in Howard 1990, p. 135)

While such a statement is a useful as a starting point, it cannot be held in mind as a single unit. To galvanize attention and action most effectively, visions must be boiled down to their essential elements in the form of *vision statements.*

Although visions are as varied as snowflakes, vision statements that are inspiring and motivating share certain characteristics:

- *Brevity.* Vision statements should be brief so that they can be easily and frequently communicated. This also allows the use of posters and buttons to reinforce the message of the vision. But brevity should not overrule the endeavor to state the vision definitively.
- *Clarity.* The degree of clarity or precision of the vision statement influences how well it is understood and accepted. Clear statements make the overarching goals understandable to everyone.
- *Abstractness.* At first glance, the criteria of clarity and abstractness may appear to be contradictory. This is not the case, however, because *abstract,* as the word is used here, simply means that the vision should represent a general ideal as opposed to a specific achievement. A vision is not a narrow, one-time goal that can be met, then discarded.
- *Challenge.* A vision is an idea that motivates people to work toward a desirable outcome; therefore, it must be inherently

challenging. Visions challenge people to do their best. In fact, Bennis and Nanus found that "attention through vision" was a key strategy used by the leaders they interviewed: "The visions these various leaders conveyed seemed to bring about a confidence on the part of the employees, a confidence that instilled in them a belief that they were capable of performing the necessary acts" (1985, p. 30).

- *Future-orientation.* By definition, visions are future-oriented. Visions should focus on the long-term perspective of the organization and the environment in which it functions. The vision should guide the organization far into the future. James Houghton of Corning Glass Ware espouses a vision of "quality" and says, "Quality applies to everything we do. This is a life-long journey, not a destination" (quoted in Labich 1988, p. 63).

- *Stability.* Visions typically do not change frequently or dramatically (Gabarro 1987; Tichy and Devanna 1986). They are general and abstract enough that they are not affected by most of the changes in the market or in technology. When changes must be made in the vision statement, they should only be minor adjustments to reflect changes in the operating environment (Peters 1987). Occasionally, an entirely new vision statement is required, but only if the organization needs to undergo a significant transformation.

- *Desirability.* Perhaps the most important criterion of a vision is the desirability of attaining it. Followers must view the vision as an ideal that is worth working toward. If followers do not perceive the vision as an attractive goal, they will never commit themselves to achieving it—and the leader will be unable to lead.

Examples of visions that fit many of the above criteria are that of Stewart Bainum, Jr., president of Manor Care, and that of florist Podesta Baldocci. At Manor Care, Bainum says, the vision centers on becoming "the best nursing care system in the world" (quoted in Ackoff 1978). Baldocci's vision is one of "selling beauty," not just flowers (Kouzes and Posner 1987). Both visions are abstract, compared with one specifying an exact achievement of, for example, a 25 percent increase in sales in two years. Both visions are challenging, and both are designed to foster an environment of constant improvement—whether that improvement is realized through improved patient care or more creative floral arrangements. These visions can guide their organizations long into the future and may never need to be replaced because of their general yet inspiring focus. Further, because of the comparative nature of Bainum's vision, as long as there is competition in the nursing-care business, the vision will continue to be challenging. Finally, because of the type of person who is attracted to the work in a nursing home, it is reasonable to expect employees to accept that vision as desirable.

Formulating the Vision

Although leaders ultimately formulate a company's vision, they often seek information from outside sources while they are developing it. Leaders choose an image from those available at the moment, articulate it, give it form and legitimacy, and focus attention on it, but they do not conceive it out of thin air (Bennis and Nanus 1985; Tichy and Devanna 1986). Each step of the formulation process may be influenced by information and the opinions of knowledgeable individuals.

Formulating the vision requires that leaders

- gather information,
- process the information,
- conceptualize their vision, and
- evaluate the vision.

Gathering information or monitoring the environment, is the first stage in vision formulation (Bennis and Nanus 1985; Gabarro 1987). Accessing different sources of information both inside and outside the organization is essential because it exposes a leader to a variety of perspectives and points of view.

Gathering information requires the leader to talk to and *listen to* the different people in the organization. When Bainum returned to Manor Care, the company his father had founded, he was faced with the task of formulating a vision. His primary strategy was to talk to employees. Both in informal conversations and in formal management committee meetings, he asked, "What's wrong, and what's right?" The answers he received highlighted the problems that existed in the corporation and helped him form the vision of creating "the best nursing care system in the world" (Bainum 1989). It is crucial that a leader seek information from within the organization before formulating a vision.

It is equally important that leaders monitor the larger organizational environment, utilizing previously developed networks. Kouzes and Posner (1987) call this gaining "outsight." External sources of information can provide unique perspectives that organizational insiders may lack. Leaders need to be aware of the trends, changes, and needs in their industry. Networking, reading, attending lectures and conferences, and talking with industry experts, customers, and suppliers are a few ways in which leaders gather information relevant to their organizations.

George Hatsopoulos of Thermo Electron believes in the value of learning as much as possible about his environment. In an interview with *Inc.* magazine, he remarked, "The more you understand the overall environment—and really, it's the whole world—the better able you'll be to find the opportunities" (quoted in Posner and Solomon 1988, p. 30). Hatsopoulos bases this belief on his personal experience. He notes that a process of information-gathering allows him—and consequently his company—to anticipate and meet future needs in the industry. Knowing the value of being well-informed, he makes a concerted effort to gather information by keeping in touch with members of Congress, government agencies, and other companies in the industry as well as by researching specific concerns through extensive reading.

Processing information requires the leader to analyze and synthesize all the information obtained from as many sources as possible to form the vision for his or her organization. Cognitive ability is clearly important here. This stage also may require a great deal of time and even creativity. Bennis and Nanus propose, "If there is a spark of genius in the leadership function at all, it must lie in this transcending ability, a kind of magic, to assemble—out of all the variety of images, signals, forecasts and alternatives—a clearly articulated vision of the future that is at once simple, easily understood, clearly desirable, and energizing" (1985, p. 103).

They further counsel that synthesizing a vision requires

- *foresight,* to ensure that the vision will be appropriate for the future environment;
- *hindsight,* so that organizational tradition and culture are not overly violated;
- *a worldview,* to capitalize on the impact of new developments and trends;
- *depth perception,* to see the whole picture in detail and perspective;
- *peripheral vision,* to foresee possible responses from competitors; and
- *a process of revision,* so that the vision reflects and will continue to reflect changes in the environment. (1985, pp. 102–103)

Despite these requirements, analyzing and synthesizing information to form a vision requires more than conscious information-processing. It also requires intuition. *Intuition* (in the nonmystical sense) refers to the knowledge and values stored in one's subconscious, and it is usually based on years of experience.

Kouzes and Posner (1987) describe intuition as the wellspring of vision. Intuition also depends on the ability to picture and imagine. Experience is the base of intuition that, in turn, helps people to gain perspective on new information. Lee Iacocca, for example, relied more on his intuition than on staff reports when he was developing a new vision for Chrysler (cited in Bennis and Nanus 1985).

Leaders need to know their organizations intimately. Their experience and intuition can then help them to analyze and integrate the information they have gathered. When processing information, some of the questions leaders should ask themselves are:

- Is this information relevant to my organization?
- Based on my experience with the people in this organization, will the proposed approach work?
- What effect can I anticipate that these actions would have in my organization?
- Will this approach help me achieve my goals?

Conceptualizing the vision requires the leader to generate ways to express the vision statement. Initially, the leader may need to generate several alternatives that can be tested later during evaluation of the vision. As we have seen, the vision statement should be brief, clear, abstract, challenging, future-oriented, stable, and desirable to those individuals who will be working to achieve it. The vision statement must motivate everyone to work toward the organization's goals.

Evaluating the vision is the final step in formulating a vision. It is important to test and revise the vision before implementing it on a large scale. During the process of developing a vision, ideas should be stated and restated in an effort to discover the best, most accurate articulation of the vision, taking into consideration the different nuances that certain words convey.

It is also important to evaluate the usefulness and appropriateness of the vision. Hickman and Silva suggest the use of mental scenarios:

> Once you have meditated on the crucial questions about your organization and its environment, you can take the next important step, mentally creating the future before you create it physically. At some point during your meditations, you will leave the world of introspection for the world of *projection*. Because projection provides a means for testing your vision before you fully commit your company to it, it begins even before a fuzzy vision resolves into a clear picture. Obviously, the more mistakes you can avoid during testing, the better your chances for ultimate success. Mentally creating the future through scenario building clarifies initial fuzziness and minimizes costly trial and error. (1984, p. 168)

A good vision statement guides the organization successfully through both minor changes in the organization and major changes in the industry. But even after a vision has been formulated, it is important that the leader continue to gather, analyze, and integrate information and to continue to evaluate the appropriateness of the vision. Such vigilance will signal any need for a change in the vision statement. Questions the leader should use to periodically evaluate the vision are:

- Does this vision accurately articulate our goals?
- Is the vision consistent with our actual capabilities?

If the answer to either of these questions is no, then the vision needs to be modified to better reflect the current direction and potential of the organization. Because of the stable and future-oriented nature of a properly developed vision, changes should be few. In most cases, the changes needed will be only minor alterations that allow the vision to continue to evolve to reflect the needs of the environment.

Once a well-informed leader has a thoroughly considered and tested vision statement, it is time to present (or re-present) it to the organization's employees and to work to gain their commitment to it.

Promoting Commitment to the Vision

The leader's next and perhaps most critical challenge is to instill the vision in others (Kouzes and Posner 1987). Before a leader can hope to achieve the vision, he or she must work to clarify the vision for the followers and build their commitment to it. Without follower commitment, nothing is accomplished. Commitment is obtained first through the process of communication.

Communicating the message of the vision is crucial because without effective communication, that message remains hidden and impotent. Leaders must be able to explain the vision in clear terms so that the followers can understand, accept, and commit to that vision. They must be able to make every employee see how the vision is relevant to his or her job and how the vision can be achieved. As Bennis and Nanus state, "The leader may generate new views of the future and may be a genius at synthesizing and articulating them, but this makes a difference only when the vision has been successfully communicated throughout the organization and effectively institutionalized as a guiding principle. Leaders are only as powerful as the ideas they can communicate" (1985, pp. 106–107).

The process of communication includes stating the vision, stating its purpose or value, and explaining the ways in which the vision will guide organizational activities. Leaders communicate this information through speeches, meetings, memos, newsletters, and conversations that emphasize the importance of the vision. Rallying cries, metaphors, slogans, buttons, posters, stories, and ceremonies can be used effectively to instill the vision in others. Indeed, the vision should implicitly direct all organizational activities.

It is vitally important to make sure that daily information about the vision and the short-term goals that will be used to help implement it are clearly communicated to all levels of the organization (Bass 1985; Tichy and Devanna 1986). One assembly worker's remark illustrates what happens when this is not done: "Sometimes, top management sees an apple. When it gets to middle management, it's an orange. By the time it gets to us, it's a lemon" (quoted in Kouzes and Posner 1987, p. 100).

Making the vision personally relevant and inspiring to each person in the organization is necessary if the vision is to be energizing. Individuals will not work to achieve a vision if they do not accept it, and people cannot be made to accept a vision through coercion or by simply asking them to "come aboard." A leader must convince the individuals to align themselves with the organization's vision by generating enthusiasm for the vision and by showing them how their interests can be served by implementing it.

Hickman and Silva (1984) suggest that leaders work to translate the vision into a reason for being for each employee by continually relating the vision to their individual cares, concerns, and work. Appealing to shared values may help show followers how their interests can be served by the vision. For example, Manor Care's vision of being the best nursing-care system in the world has a potentially strong employee appeal because health-care professionals are likely to identify with its implied message of helping others and with its expressed desire to excel.

One way leaders generate enthusiasm for their vision is by being enthusiastic and positive about it themselves. Kouzes and Posner maintain, "Leaders cannot ignite the flame of passion in their followers if they themselves do not express enthusiasm for the compelling vision of the group" (1987, p. 10). Emotional appeals may also help inspire followers to believe in the vision and generate enthusiasm (Bass 1985; Kouzes and Posner 1987). For instance, florist Podesta Baldocci's vision of selling beauty, not flowers, appeals to employees on an emotional level.

Phil Turner, the former facilities manager for Raychem Corporation who was later promoted to plant manager for Raychem's Wire and Cable Division, describes the division's purpose in the following way: "Our job is to lift people's spirits through beauty, cleanliness, and functionality, enthusiasm, good cheer, and excellence" (quoted in Kouzes and Posner 1987, p. 83). Turner made the hot-air balloon the symbol of the facility's operation.

Lisa Foley, president and CEO of Canton Industrial Corporation, a firm that produces mailboxes, illustrates her vision similarly: "I want to make Canton, Illinois, the mailbox capital of the world. I can see a little sign as you enter town: 'Welcome to Canton, the mailbox capital of the world'" (quoted in Kouzes and Posner 1987, p. 92).

Taking action becomes the focus after the vision has been clearly communicated and made personally relevant for each employee. The leader is faced with the ongoing task of demonstrating what actions are consistent with the vision.

Role modeling may be the most effective way for the leader to provide examples of desired actions and modes of behavior (Peters 1987). Suppose Company XYZ's vision, for example, is to "provide the best service in the industry." To instill this vision in all employees, the company's CEO might take an active and highly visible role in providing quality service by personally responding to customer complaints. Employees would then understand exactly what the vision means in reality.

By acting in accord with the vision, leaders also communicate to followers the importance of the vision and their own commitment to it. It is important for leaders to practice what they preach: "Managers may speak eloquently about the vision and values, but if their behavior is not consistent with their stated beliefs, people ultimately will lose respect for them" (Kouzes and Posner 1987, p. 12).

Other leadership actions can show the importance of the vision. Stewart Bainum of Manor Care, for instance, reduced his contract nursing staff and increased the number of nurses working directly for Manor Care. He did this to ensure the best-quality care in the company's nursing facilities, despite the higher costs associated with directly employing more nurses. This demonstrated to all of Manor Care's employees that quality care was the top priority.

Only after understanding of, acceptance of, and commitment to the vision have begun to grow can the leader expect to successfully implement it. To do this, however, the leader also needs a plan or strategy.

Developing a Strategic Vision

A vision represents a relatively stable, overarching organizational goal. Once stated, such goals don't just happen. Achieving them requires planning. A strategic vision is an overarching plan for achieving the overarching goal. It is the "strategic thrust" of the organization.

Entrepreneur Steve Bostic emphasizes that growth must "be planned. You have to take your vision, think it through, and turn it into a consistent strategy." Further, Bostic stresses, "a vision doesn't amount to much if you can't develop a strategy and an organization to achieve it" (quoted in Gendron and Burlingham 1989, pp. 47–48).

A successful strategic vision takes into account the industry, the customers, and the specific competitive environment in order to identify an innovation targeted at a particular competitive position that will help the organization carve out a unique place for itself in the industry (Pearson 1989).

Bainum's strategic plan for Manor Care meets the criteria of a successful strategic vision. His plan considered the nursing-care industry, an industry in which the limited financial resources of clients typically plagues most nursing homes. Bainum's plan targeted upper-income people who are in need of nursing-care services, a strategy consistent with Manor Care's vision of providing the best-quality nursing care. This strategy defined Manor Care's competitive position (Bainum 1989).

When Ned Johnson took over Fidelity Management and Research, he identified the need for a strategic vision. The mutual-fund industry was generally characterized by poor service and a "one-shot" mentality. If a fund did not do well in a particular quarter, customers traditionally moved elsewhere. "Johnson envisioned a supermarket of 50 to 60 funds that would offer customers every conceivable investment focus plus superior service" (Pearson 1989, p. 96). Implementing this strategy made it easy for Fidelity to retain customers, who could switch to a better-performing fund without going to a competitor.

David Farrell's strategic vision allowed him to turn May Department Stores into one of the nation's largest, best-run publicly held department-store chains. Instead of diversifying out of the department-store business, as he had been advised and as competitors were doing, Farrell "centralized merchandising concepts, priced aggressively, eliminated loser departments, built strong execution-driven local managements and got control of costs" (Pearson 1989, p. 97).

In all of these examples, strategic planning provided the necessary thrust to direct organizational activities in the direction of the vision.

Summary

The vision should be the primary guiding force of all organizational activity. A leader's key function is to develop that vision. After translating it into a precise and succinct vision statement, the leader must convince followers that working to implement the vision is in their best interests and must provide them with a strategic plan for that implementation.

The next chapter explores the extraordinarily complex process of implementing the vision.

5

Implementation of the Vision

A leader who is motivated, skilled, and visionary—but nothing more—will remain simply a motivated, skilled dreamer. Real leaders use their motives, traits, and skills to actualize their vision in reality by taking the steps necessary to implement it.

A leader's first implementation step is to translate the vision into an *agenda*—a list of things to be done. Agendas are the link between a vision and its implementation; through them a leader creates a reality-based guide for achieving the vision of an organization.

Agendas have been found to be central to the way managers structure work. Harvard's John Kotter (1982) describes the typical general manager's agenda as "a set of loosely connected goals and plans." These agendas are

- comprised of short, medium, and long-term responsibilities;
- typically broad and unwritten;
- primarily developed during the first six months;
- formed in increments; and
- closely intertwined with the manager's networking activities.

The managers rarely have a clear agenda when they first begin their jobs, Kotter reports, but they use their preliminary knowledge of their organizations, along with new information they receive every day, to quickly develop a tentative agenda. This agenda is incrementally adjusted over time through the addition of information until it becomes more specific and complete. The managers

Chapter 5 was written mainly by Jodi Schneider, Harold Goldstein, and Kurt Welsh.

obtain the information they need to create the more-complete agenda through their own observations and through frequent discussions with others in the organization.

Some leaders suggest that limiting an agenda is crucial to the effectiveness of an organization. Dr. William Kirwan, president of the University of Maryland at College Park, for example, states that the agenda must be limited because a leader cannot handle too many things at once. An agenda with too many items can overwhelm an organization to the point that it is paralyzed and unable to achieve anything.

To repeat, agendas are the link between the organizational vision and its implementation by organization members. The sequence progresses from vision to agendas to specific policies and procedures. The specific policies and procedures required to implement a vision typically fall into six categories:

- structuring,
- selecting, training, and acculturating employees,
- motivating employees,
- managing information,
- team building, and
- promoting change.

Structuring

Structuring, or designing, the organization is crucial for determining how and whether the vision of the organization will be achieved. Tom Peters (1987) stresses simplicity as the most important characteristic of structure. He points to multiple layers of management and excessive bureaucracy as major causes of problems in organizations. Excessive organizational complexity and formality, for example, are principal causes of slow corporate responsiveness to a changing environment.

Bureaucratic organizational structures also reduce the autonomy and responsibility of the organization's members (Bennis and Nanus 1985; Gardner 1986–88; Pearson 1989; Schein 1985; Tichy and Devanna 1986; Yukl 1989). In addition, an excessive number of layers in an organization inhibits the flow of information, especially upward and diagonal communications.

To simplify organizational structure, Peters (1987) recommends the following:

- Radically reduce the number of layers of management.
- Keep central staff very small.
- Assign most support staff to the field.
- Establish a wide span of control.

With respect to reducing the layers of management, Peters recommends five levels of hierarchy as the absolute maximum. To back up his recommendation of layer limitation, he cites a study conducted by management consultant A. T. Kearney that compared forty-one large companies on the basis of long-term financial performance. The companies that performed well averaged nearly four fewer layers of management than companies that did not, and they had approximately five-hundred fewer central staff specialists per $1 billion sales. In addition, Peters cites a study by McKinsey and Company that examined thirty-eight advanced manufacturing technology systems and concluded that the first step in improving productivity is to clean out layers of middle management and support staff that clog the wheels of change.

Peters also recommends assigning the most support staff to the field. This creates a climate of "business-mindedness" that is geared to successful performance in the workplace rather than to preoccupation with corporate ladder-climbing and political maneuvering. A successful example of this practice is Mars, Inc., in which a thirty-person headquarters guides a $7 billion company. Mars executives suggest that their company's effectiveness "stems from their placement of virtually all staff people in factories, sales branches, and distribution centers. They do not populate corporate or other central headquarters" (Peters 1987, p. 431).

Peters's final recommendation is to establish a wide span of control. This means that the organization should increase the ratio of nonsupervisors to supervisors at the organization's front lines. The broadening of the span of control will result in a hierarchy that has fewer levels between its highest and lowest members. Peters recommends that minimum spans of control at the front line be one supervisor for every twenty-five to seventy-five nonsupervisors.

This structure is not common in practice, however. When James O'Toole studied spans of control, he observed a typical ratio of one supervisor to ten nonsupervisors in the United States (cited in Peters 1987). He noted that the Japanese ratios are approximately one to one hundred and concluded that American workers are oversupervised.

Simplifying organizational structure pushes responsibility downward (an issue covered in more detail later), and decreases the likelihood that changes recommended from below will be vetoed or diluted from above. It also increases the ability of the organization to respond rapidly to changes in the business environment, such as changes in competitors' actions and customers' needs.

Robert D. Haas, CEO of Levi Strauss & Co., perceives that an "enormous diffusion of power" is becoming common—and necessary—in the organizational structures of corporations. "If companies are going to react quickly to changes in the marketplace, they have to put more and more accountability, authority, and information into the hands of people who are closest to the product and the customers" (quoted in Howard 1990, p. 134).

Selecting, Acculturating, and Training Employees

Selecting and developing followers who are capable and willing to work toward achieving the organization's vision is an important leadership task because leaders depend on followers to achieve goals. The selection process lays the groundwork for the efficient running of the organization, and a leader must therefore choose employees carefully. Only if a leader has selected employees with the "right stuff" will he or she have the resources to achieve the organization's vision.

Effective leaders must invest heavily in employee selection and utilize an extensive recruitment process, regardless of the time and resources that that may require. The best recruiting is accomplished by firms that have straightforward recruitment objectives. An obvious objective is to select employees who have the abilities the job requires. Salespersons, for example, must have the ability to communicate, and computer programmers must know computer language and possess mathematical abilities. A second recruitment objective is to choose employees who will fit into the organizational culture. At Nordstrom, a regional vice president indicates that prior experience is not as important in a new employee as interpersonal skills. Retailer Luciano Bennetton looks for employees with the "right spirit" when recruiting. Both of these companies have been highly successful with employee management.

Acculturating is the process by which an organization's culture and vision are instilled in individual members. Leaders must make provisions for this process. One way to acculturate employees is through the recruitment process itself, and new employees are the easiest to acculturate. As Peters notes, "A lengthy set of interviews unmistakably demonstrates that the firm cares enough about the candidate and the working environment to get people at all levels deeply involved in recruitment. Those that are hired start with the key values . . . instilled by the recruitment process itself" (1987, p. 382).

To acculturate followers, leaders should articulate their vision into an easy-to-grasp philosophy that integrates strategic direction and cultural values. Leaders must motivate employees to embrace the vision through constant persuasion, by setting an example, and by relating the vision to individual needs and concerns (Hickman and Silva 1984).

It is important for leaders to acculturate management personnel as well as lower-level employees. For example, General Motors president Roger Smith once took his top nine hundred executives on a five-day retreat to share and discuss his vision for the future of GM, and the executives were expected to affirm their commitment to that vision (cited in Bennis and Nanus 1985).

In fact, a leader must be particularly concerned with acculturating those in the highest positions. These are people who will need to carry on the vision after the leader is gone. By acculturating top management, the leader ensures that the vision will endure. J. Willard Marriott of Marriott Corporation and Tom Watson of IBM both groomed their sons to take over, while Ray Kroc of McDonald's chose Fred Turner to succeed him because "he was in the Kroc mold" (quoted in Smith and Harrison 1986, pp. 27–28).

Training is required to help members of the organization learn where they fit in with the organization's vision and goals, the particular responsibilities and duties of their positions, what is expected of them, and how their performance will be measured. Further, they must be helped to develop the specific skills that their jobs require now and will require in the future. Not even an elaborate selection process can eliminate the need for such training.

In recognition of the importance of training, corporations are beginning to allocate more resources to it. Some years ago Motorola, for example, increased its spending on employee training to $100 million annually to help achieve its vision of quality (Hillkirk 1989).

When Citicorp studied a number of companies that were considered to be tops in rendering customer service, it found that most spent one to two percent of their sales on training front-line employees. William Davidow and Bro Uttal (1989) pinpoint "training—constant, intensive, lavish, and universal"—as an important factor in the success of these companies.

Extensive entry-level training should concentrate on the skills most important to the firm. Those skills must be carefully identified. Grocer Stew Leonard, for instance, focuses on "communication and courtesy skills" rather than just on "running a cash register" (quoted in Peters 1987). Regular retraining sessions are also needed to maintain and update employee skills and to create a career orientation—as opposed to a just-a-job mentality—for employees. This helps ensure that everyone is capable of adding value to the firm.

Acculturation and training can be combined to some extent. Training sessions provide excellent opportunities to teach values and the vision. Peters states that "the best training programs . . . must be seen as a prime opportunity to underscore [the organization's] values" (1987, p. 394).

At Levi Strauss, a comprehensive ongoing training program has been established to communicate corporate values. The program focuses on a "leadership week" course in which twenty managers at a time are taught how to implement behaviors outlined in the company's aspirations (or vision) statement. By the end of 1990, the top seven hundred people in the company had completed the course during its first twenty sessions. At each session, at least one of the company's top eight executives participated, "to send the signal of how important this is to us," reports CEO Haas (quoted in Howard 1990, p. 139).

The leadership-research literature provides support for the importance of formal training. Jay Conger (1989) finds that a lack of training support and resources leads to feelings of powerlessness among workers. Leaders need to determine areas where training is needed and provide it to develop employees capable of exemplary work. Effective leaders empower followers by helping them develop their skills, abilities, and knowledge. Bernard Bass argues that truly transformational leaders have a developmental orientation toward their subordinates: "They assign tasks on an individual basis to help subordinates alter [improve] their abilities and motivations" (1985, p. 85).

The results of such training can be dramatic. At GM's Lakewood, Georgia, plant, for example, Manager Patricia Carrigan implemented the following strategies to turn around the declining performance of the plant: pre-startup training classes, greater participation encouraged by labor in managing the plant, and an ongoing training program—dubbed "Lakewood University"—established in an unused portion of the building (cited in Kouzes and Posner 1987). Productivity and plant performance were greatly enhanced after implementing this additional training.

Training practices such as these, when combined with the proper selection of employees, can help ensure a high level of employee skill.

Motivating

Because leaders cannot achieve their vision on their own, they must motivate others to work toward it as well. An organization's employees are its most valuable asset and are the key way that organizations achieve their goals. Psychologist Gary Yukl defines the task of motivating as generating "enthusiasm for the work, commitment to task objectives, and compliance with orders and requests" (1989, p. 135). John Gardner (1986–88) describes the task of motivating as unlocking or channeling the existing motives of followers.

Although the vision itself is a powerful motivating force for individuals, it is not sufficient for sustaining high effort on a continuing basis or when obstacles and problems surface. As Kouzes and Posner explain, "The climb to the top is arduous and long. People become exhausted, frustrated, and disenchanted. They are often tempted to give up. Leaders must encourage . . . their followers to carry on" (1987, p.12).

Effective leaders motivate their followers through the use of formal authority, role modeling, building self-confidence, creating challenge through goal-setting, delegating, and rewarding and punishing.

Formal authority is inherent in the position of a leader in an organization's formal hierarchy, and it is in itself a source of motivation for followers. The fact that the leader has a higher rank in the company than the followers or is "the boss" helps the leader generate desired actions. This response is based on "legitimate power": power stemming from one's official authority (Yukl 1989).

Yukl (1989) suggests that legitimate power carries with it the implicit right of leaders to make requests of their subordinates. Peters (1987) concurs, saying that if a leader wants something, he or she should start by just asking for it. He provides a good example of a leader who uses formal authority effectively:

> A bank president called a two-day meeting at a remote location to work with his top forty officers on some strategic issues. The group trundled off at one point for a "breakout session, where teams traditionally get together to noodle over some key issues, coming back with a vague report about the important parameters." This time the president's guidance was unconventional: "You've got two hours to come up with big savings, without layoffs. . . . See you in 120 minutes." They did return—and with the savings. A significant share of ideas were implementable. (1987, p. 309)

This simple way of gaining compliance is often overlooked, perhaps because of the prevalent view that good leaders should not "just shout out orders." Many successful leaders, however, are skilled at giving orders and making requests based on their authority in ways that foster teamwork and collaboration (Kotter 1982; Kouzes and Posner 1987). Legitimate power can be effective not only because individuals have an internalized belief that they should do what the boss asks, but also because the leader's position is linked to other motivators. Power is inherent in the executive role because leaders have the authority to allocate rewards and punishments to their subordinates. (This is discussed in more detail below.)

Role modeling is another way that leaders can motivate others to work toward realizing the vision. Leaders serving as role models become visible symbols of what they want their followers to be (Kotter 1982). Kouzes and Posner state that "leaders model the way; . . . by the clarity and courage of their convictions and by their everyday actions, they demonstrate to others how visions can be realized" (1987, p. 189).

The best way for leaders to get a vision across to people is to live it themselves. Leaders cannot serve as role models through what they say alone; they also must set an example by what they do. Kouzes and Posner assert that "managers may speak eloquently about vision and values, but if their behavior is not consistent with their stated beliefs, people will ultimately lose respect for them" (1987, p. 12).

Haas at Levi Strauss emphasizes the importance of putting this into practice:

> The first responsibility for me and my team is to examine critically our own behaviors and management styles in relation to the behaviors and values that we profess to work toward becoming more consistent with the values that we are articulating. . . . you can't be one thing and say another. People have unerring detections systems for fakes, and they won't put up with them. They won't put values into practice if you're not. (Howard 1990, pp. 138-39)

When Citicorp was trying to improve its customer service, it studied the practices of a number of companies that ranked tops in service and found that the CEOs "for the most part were deeply and personally involved in the customer service function of their business. They personally read complaint logs and letters, took phone calls, and were highly visible and available to the rank and file" (cited in Davidow and Uttal 1989, p. 98).

The importance of role modeling to effective leadership has been documented consistently in the leadership literature (Bennis and Nanus 1985; Conger 1989; Gabarro 1987). Role modeling, by showing subordinates what to do, is actually a method of training; it promotes learning by example (Manz and Sims 1989). The successful leader sets examples and engages in symbolic behavior that tells followers what is expected of them, as well as which behaviors are appropriate and acceptable (Kouzes and Posner 1987; Yukl 1989).

Gabarro (1987) suggests that subordinates look to their manager's behavior for cues that indicate what is expected of them as well as what lies ahead for the group. He describes how one new general manager's working hours signaled his expectations to his employees: "He was the first one in the office. His car was in the lot by 7:00 A.M. every morning and he never left before 6:00 P.M. That told people a lot about what he expected from us" (1987, p. 87).

Effective leaders use role modeling not only to show followers what is expected of them but to communicate clearly to their followers their own commitment. At Manor Care, for example, President Bainum served as a role model to demonstrate the importance of achieving his vision of providing the highest quality nursing-care service. In a program designated Quality Awareness Week, Bainum and his management team spent an entire week away from the office performing every job at the day-care centers—from serving food to caring for patients (Bainum 1989).

Phillip Cooper, president of Davis-Edwards Limited, demonstrated his commitment to building a firm that cares by visiting twenty-seven cities in six months to meet with customers face to face (Peters 1987).

Role modeling is a powerful technique for embedding and reinforcing the organizational culture (Schein 1985). A leader can use role modeling to affirm an important organizational value, such as quality service, in various ways: by starting every meeting with a quality review, by regularly calling people at all levels of the organization to ask questions about quality, and by asking individuals to send in reports on some aspect of quality in their organization (Peters 1987).

Effective leaders make use of routine, day-to-day activities to model their vision, values, and expectations (Gabarro 1987). Subordinates know what is important to their leaders and their organizations by observing how leaders spend their time, the questions they ask, their reactions to critical incidents, and the behaviors they reward (Kouzes and Posner 1987; Peters 1987).

Peters (1987) argues that to produce organizational changes of any kind, leaders must make noticeable changes in the way they themselves spend their time. Leaders can preach that they want their organization to become more innovative, for example, but it is the message in their actions that ultimately determines whether their subordinates engage in innovative behaviors. Employees watch to see how much time the leader spends addressing innovation issues:

- Is innovation the number-one item on the leader's agenda?
- Does the leader attend conferences on the latest innovations in the business?
- Is an employee who develops a new product rewarded?
- What are the leader's reactions to innovative behavior that results in positive or negative consequences for the organization?

Building self-confidence instills in followers a belief that they have the capacity to perform their jobs successfully and to contribute to achieving the organization's vision. As Gardner states, "leaders must help people believe that they can be effective, that their goals are possible for accomplishment, that there is a better future that they can move toward through their own efforts" (1989, p. 4). Because leaders possess self-confidence themselves (see Chapter 2), they have an advantage when trying to build and develop the self-confidence of their followers (Bennis and Nanus 1985).

Building self-confidence is one way that leaders empower their followers. Empowerment involves strengthening an individual's own belief in his or her effectiveness (Conger 1989). When empowered, followers feel strong, powerful, and capable.

Joe Paterno, head coach of Pennsylvania State University's football team, recognizes the empowering effect of confidence-building:

When the staff is down . . . when the squad is down . . . when they are starting to doubt themselves . . . then it's gotta be a positive approach. The minute I have the feeling they have doubts concerning . . . [their] ability to do it . . . then I immediately want to jump in there and . . . talk about how good the kids are and what a great job they've done. (quoted in Manz and Sims 1989, p. 72)

The leadership role of confidence-building is critical to achieving a company's vision because feelings of self-confidence may determine whether followers will attempt the vision journey in the first place and whether they will give up when faced with setbacks. Self-confident followers exert greater effort in achieving the goals set forth by the vision, and they experience better performance. Conversely, a loss of confidence results in "an incapacity to summon energy on behalf of purposeful effort, an unwillingness to take risks, and a fatal timidity when the moment of opportunity breaks" (Gardner 1989, p. 5).

The effect of instilling a sense of self-confidence in others is referred to as the Pygmalion effect. It has been shown repeatedly that people who are led to expect that they will do well do better than those who are led to expect they will do poorly (Bass 1985; Bennis and Nanus 1985; Eden 1990; Kouzes and Posner 1987; Manz and Sims 1989). Leaders who expect high performance strengthen their followers' beliefs regarding the relationship between the followers' efforts and successful performance. As a result, followers are more likely to exert the effort required for successful performance. Advocates of the Pygmalion effect argue for using techniques that deliberately raise the expectations of others to increase their work motivation (Eden 1990). Leaders can enhance the self-confidence of their followers most directly by communicating a belief in their ability to succeed (Bass 1985; Kouzes and Posner 1987).

Effective leaders spend a significant amount of their time expressing confidence in their subordinate's abilities. They do so on a daily basis—in speeches, in meetings, and in casual interactions with others.

Renn Zaphiropoulos, president and CEO of Versatec, exemplifies how effective leaders build the self-confidence of their followers. When his employees told him that they wanted to develop a new machine in five months instead of the projected two-and-a-half years, Zaphiropoulos replied, "That is a wonderful idea," instead of debunking their enthusiasm by telling them it was a "crazy idea" (Kouzes and Posner 1987, p. 43).

The inspiration that a supervisor can provide in building confidence in others is described by one employee this way:

> My supervisor held a meeting to talk about how vital the new contract is for the company and said he was confident we could handle it if we all did our part.
> My boss told us we were the best design group he had ever worked

with and he was sure that this new product was going to break every sales record in the company. (Yukl, 1987, p. 121)

Delegating may at first seem to require giving up some of the authority that rests with leadership, but contrary to the stereotype of an all-powerful leader, successful leaders recognize that "power is an expandable pie" (Kouzes and Posner 1987, p. 162). Delegation gives responsibility and a degree of autonomy to followers. Tasks from problem-diagnosis to decision-making to leadership functions are delegated within successful organizations (House 1988).

Delegation helps to empower followers (Conger, 1989). The process of empowering requires a leader to be able to transform followers into partial leaders (Kouzes and Posner 1987). Charles Manz and Henry Sims (1989) challenge traditional assumptions about leadership practices in their discussion of "SuperLeadership." Superleaders "lead others to lead themselves," and, the authors note, "the principal means of establishing the commitment and enthusiasm necessary to achieve long-term excellence in an organization is to unleash the self-leadership potential within each person (1989, pp. 5, 7).

Delegation is also a strategy that enriches jobs. Job enrichment involves restructuring jobs with the intention of making them more challenging, motivating, and rewarding to the individual. Hackman and Oldham's (1976) Job Characteristics Model is one of the leading theoretical frameworks for developing and implementing job-enrichment programs. The model proposes that there are five core job characteristics that result in employee motivation:

- autonomy,
- task significance,
- skill variety,
- task identity, and
- feedback.

Consistent with the job-enrichment approach is the suggestion that leaders should enhance the natural rewards of their subordinates' tasks—the rewarding properties of their jobs in and of themselves—and even encourage employees to redesign their own jobs to be more rewarding (Manz and Sims 1989). Manz and Sims also contend that when individuals take on new jobs that offer more responsibility and autonomy, they may be motivated to do the work for its own sake. Numerous studies have found a positive relationship between job enrichment and positive organizational outcomes (Locke, Sirota, and Wolfson 1976; Umstot, Bell, and Mitchell 1976).

True delegation does not entail simply handing over tasks and passing out assignments routinely. It requires empowering followers with true ownership and with the true burden of responsibility. True delegation involves "really letting go," which is accomplished through such practices as relatively infrequent formal reporting, geographic separation, and psychological distancing. Leaders who truly delegate not only ask subordinates for their input but give them the ultimate responsibility for making decisions. Moreover, delegation is effective only if followers are given responsibility over something that is relevant to "the pressing concerns and core technology of the business. Choosing the color of the paint may be a place to start, but [a leader] had better give people influence over more substantive issues" (Kouzes and Posner 1987, p. 182).

Gordon Forward of Chaparral Steel provides an example of true delegation. Chaparral Steel produces steel of high quality, but they have no quality inspectors. "Our people in the plants are responsible for their own products and its quality. . . . We expect them to act like owners" suggests Forward (quoted in Peters 1987, p. 349).

The very nature of delegation explains why many leaders fail to delegate. True delegation entails giving up control, and it is indeed risky. Yet effective leaders recognize the counterbalance of the many positive benefits of delegating responsibility, both for the organization and for themselves. Delegation increases followers' ownership of and commitment to realizing the organization's vision and goals.

A study conducted at Honeywell reveals that good managers are not born but can be cultivated within a company (cited in Manz and Sims 1989, p. 9). Two recommendations related to delegation were suggested: Important projects should be delegated to subordinates, and subordinates should be involved in long-range planning.

Delegation frees a leader's time for other things. Leaders cannot possibly accomplish their most critical tasks without delegating some responsibility to their followers. By delegating, leaders also take advantage of the diverse talents and energies of individuals within the organization. Beth Pritchard, of S. C. Johnson Wax's insect-control division, attributes her success to her recognition of the potential of employees working for her. She delegates as much authority as possible (Labich 1988).

Finally, delegation is fundamentally a system of trust. Leaders signal that they trust an individual when they truly delegate authority to that person (Kouzes and Posner 1987). Leaders who refuse to delegate are seen as less trusting by their followers and correspondingly as less trustworthy. This is an important issue, because trustworthiness (discussed in Chapter 2 as part of honesty/integrity) is one of the most critical characteristics of effective leadership.

PepsiCo is a classic example of a company where delegation has had a substantial impact. PepsiCo adopted a philosophy of encouraging managers to take on responsibility and make their own decisions. The belief was that such risks would pay off. The risks did pay off in the case of manager Peter McNally, who was responsible for a $500 million branch of Frito-Lay. McNally replaced the single-serving one-ounce bags of chips with the new two-ounce grab bags. Sales have been growing 15 percent a year since the implementation of the change in 1985 (Dumaine 1989).

Although delegation has many potentially positive consequences for organizations and their members, it is not universally successful in motivating employees or increasing performance. For the delegation of decisions to be effective, there are some qualifying prerequisites: Subordinates should be competent, desire responsibility, and share the leader's objectives (Yukl 1989). Leaders must be skillful at determining when it is and is not appropriate to delegate responsibility, since delegation does not serve as an effective tool for attaining the organization's vision when employees are incompetent, poorly trained, or otherwise incapable of handling the responsibilities they are given.

Successful delegation requires setting different parameters for different individuals—and different parameters for the same individuals, when different tasks are involved. "Some people are going to be very inexperienced in certain things, so you need to be careful about setting the parameters of where they have authority and where they need to stop to seek clarification. Other people have experience, skills, and a track record, and within certain areas you want to give them a lot of latitude," suggests Levi's Robert Haas (quoted in Howard 1990, p. 135).

Delegation, while an excellent motivator, is not sufficient to guarantee successful outcomes. Delegation must be accompanied by accountability—which means responsibility for getting results—that is, for attaining specific goals.

Creating challenge through goal-setting is an indispensable means for implementing an organizational agenda and an organizational vision. It is a key method of motivating followers (as well as leaders themselves). Locke and Latham (1984, 1990) maintain, however, that to be effective motivators, goals must be not only challenging but clear and specific.

That successful leaders can be characterized as "challengers, not coddlers" became apparent to Bennis and Nanus (1985) in their study of sixty CEOs. Just how weighty the challenge should be is an issue that each leader must decide. Edwin H. Land, founder of Polaroid, made the following comment about the motivating effect of creating challenge: "The first thing you naturally do is teach the person to feel that the undertaking is manifestly important and nearly impossible. . . . That draws out the drive that makes people feel strong" (quoted in Bennis and Nanus 1985, p. 30).

By creating challenge, leaders also convey to their followers that "the sky is the limit"—that anything can be accomplished—and the followers then feel confident that they are capable of performing the necessary acts for achieving the organization's vision. As a result, "extra effort can be generated by a leader who continues to introduce new projects and new challenges in a highly flexible organization" (Bass 1985, p. 72).

To sustain morale, it is important that goal expectations not cross the fine line between being challenging and being insurmountable; leaders create productive challenges by setting goals that are difficult yet attainable.* Peters (1987) suggests that goals set for em-

---

*In laboratory studies impossible goals (if accepted) actually lead to better performance than reachable goals, but in real-life settings people want to feel a sense of accomplishment and success. Challenge can still be maintained by constantly setting goals above the level of prior attainment, in line with the Japanese principle of Kaizen, described below.

ployees should be high enough to bring out the individual's optimum performance.

Joe Paterno, head coach of Penn State's football team, also believes in setting challenging goals. He argues that "a coach has to set high goals. . . . He has to aim high, think big, and then make sure that his players aspire to the highest goals they can achieve. He has to be able to get people to reach up" (quoted in Manz and Sims 1989, p. 73).

Marshall Hahn, the very successful chairman of Georgia Pacific, says, "You always have to have [a seemingly but not actually] impossible budget and an impossible production schedule." He calls Georgia Pacific "a disciplined and friendly place" (quoted in Calonius 1990, p. 83).

Renn Zaphiropoulos of Versatec "searches for opportunities for people to exceed their previous levels of performance. He regularly sets the bar higher. And like other successful leaders, he knows that the challenge can't be so great as to be discouraging" (Kouzes and Posner 1987, p. 43).

Zaphiropoulos's approach to goal-setting is the same as that used by the Japanese, especially with respect to quality. This procedure is called *Kaizen,* which is translated as "constant improvement" (Imai 1986). Every time the Japanese attain a goal for quality, cost, or innovation, they ask themselves, How can we do it better? How can we improve? They are never satisfied with the status quo or with past attainments. Reaching a goal is merely a signal to set a higher one. Goal-setting is done in small increments so that people never become discouraged; at the same time, they are never permanently satisfied. The Japanese vision is of a never-ending quest for improvement both in work process and in outcome.

Performance improvement does not, however, have to be as gradual as the Kaizen principle implies. Motorola chairman Robert Galvin wanted a dramatic improvement in the quality of the company's products. His appointed quality director, Jack Germaine, set a goal of a tenfold increase in quality over five years. Progress was slow at first, but between 1985 and 1989 there was a 90 percent decrease in cellular phone defects. In 1988 Motorola won the coveted Malcolm Baldrige National Quality Award. The company has set even harder quality goals for 1992 (Hillkirk 1989).

Challenging goals motivate individuals to put forth high degrees of effort and persistence and also to search for more efficient and creative strategies. When individuals achieve difficult goals, they feel strong and capable of accomplishing more. They feel like "winners." The motivating effect of setting challenging goals has exemplified by the announcement that the United States would put a man on the moon within the decade. That goal was "breathtaking" and it was met, notes John Gardner. "And no one can doubt that . . . the achievement was hastened by the dramatic announcement" (1989, p. 7).

Besides creating challenge, the goal-setting process also provides followers with direction through specificity (Locke and Latham 1984, 1990). Goal-setting determines specific criteria of performance in order to encourage and direct performance to that level. By setting goals, leaders can focus their followers' attention on what they need to do. By knowing what is expected of them, followers are more likely to perform the tasks necessary for implementing the vision. Burns (1978) finds that goal-setting is useful in helping individuals focus rather than sift through broad hopes and aspirations. The ability to set goals and plan effectively is a skill that distinguishes more successful managers from those who are less successful (Boyatzis 1982).

An important question to consider when setting goals is the question of who should set them. It is the leader's job to develop the vision or overarching goal for the organization, either using or not using the input of others. But with respect to setting goals for managers and subordinates, a three-stage process is recommended:

- *Assign* goals (set by the leader) to new, inexperienced employees.
- Use *participation* (or joint goal-setting) as employees become more experienced and show some degree of competence.
- *Delegate* goal-setting (that is, let employees set their own goals) when employees become highly competent and have shown that they fully share the values of the organization.

When employees are motivated by self-set goals, they are engaging in what Manz and Sims (1989) call "self-leadership"; "superleaders" aim at developing all their employees into self-leaders.

When goal-setting is delegated, it must be constrained by the requirement of compatibility with the overarching purpose of the organization. To prevent anarchy, therefore, delegation must be accompanied by *accountability*. Obviously, an organization cannot succeed if every manager and employee goes off on a different tangent. Organizational members must be accountable for taking actions that further the vision. This means they must be accountable for attaining specific goals that are consistent with and help attain the overarching goals of the organization. In one study, service leaders were found to set "astronomically high standards for their employees and their companies" (cited in Davidow and Uttal 1989, p. 98). At Nordstrom, such accountability means that a "sales rep who receives more than one warning about falling below standard for all sorts of behavior—sales performance, appearance, attitude, customer service, or goal setting—had better look for a new job. So had an IBM employee who fails to respond to a customer emergency" (Davidow and Uttal 1989, p. 99).

To determine whether employees are reaching their goals, it is necessary that they obtain *feedback* regarding their own progress. Research shows very clearly that goal-setting does not work unless people are given information showing their performance in relation to their goals. Goals regulate performance far more reliably when feedback is present than when it is absent (Locke and Latham 1984, 1990).

It is not only followers who need feedback on goal-setting. Leaders, too, need feedback when they set goals jointly with their subordinates. Leaders must understand their followers' expectations and take them into account when setting mutually agreed-upon goals. Often, leaders must resolve discrepancies between their subordinates' expectations and their own. Gabarro (1987) finds that ineffective and unsatisfying subordinate-leader relationships are characterized by a failure of the leader to clarify, test, or work through mutual expectations. Feedback can be given to followers on the spot, through normal, daily interactions or it can be provided in formal meetings.

If feedback is necessary for goal-setting to be effective, goal-setting in turn determines the effectiveness of feedback (Locke and Latham 1990). Goals are the key mechanism by which feedback gets translated into action. If goal-setting in response to feedback does not occur, then feedback has no effect—or it has a much smaller effect—on performance. This highlights the importance of goal-setting as part of the performance-feedback process.

Assuring the validity of feedback, particularly from outside of the organization, is therefore a constant necessity. One study of customer service (Davidow and Uttal 1989) determined that neither studying customer complaints nor making sporadic random samplings gives an accurate picture of customer satisfaction. Customers who take the time to formally complain usually represent only a small percentage of all dissatisfied customers, and random samplings "don't represent a fair cross section of customers who have dealt with [the] company recently" (p. 201). Follow-ups on recent transactions were found to provide the most relevant feedback, and this is the source favored by American Express, Hewlett-Packard, and other customer-service leaders.

Yet feedback can be overdone. Working on the principle that "what gets measured gets done," as many managers do, is actually too simplistic. Managers and employees—especially those in organizations with elaborate computer-information systems—are often deluged with information. There is so much feedback that they simply do not know what to do with it all. Too often, they elect to ignore it.

It must be determined whether the feedback received requires attention and action, and whether such a response is critical to attaining the organization's vision. A more accurate phrasing of the above aphorism might be, "what gets measured *in relation to goals* gets done" (Locke and Latham 1990, p. 197).

To obtain useful and correct feedback, there must be careful *performance measurement* to assess the level of goals required for optimal performance. Leaders must set up a system in which individual employees' and managers' behavior and/or performance is objectively assessed (Locke and Latham 1984). This measurement should be based on the achievement of key performance objectives and should be formalized so that employees receive regular feedback regarding their evaluations.

Haas of Levi Strauss raises the question of just what constitutes effective performance for a manager. He answers his question by saying that "good managers mobilize the talents of subordinates, peers, and clients to further the group's goals" (quoted in Howard

1990, p. 141). With this criterion in mind, Haas bases evaluations of his managers on interviews with "anywhere from 10 to 16 people. The discussions are anonymous and confidential. And I report only trends, not isolated incidences" (quoted in Howard, 1990, p. 141). Haas talks with people who report to the manager as well as to peers and others with whom the person interacts, then gives feedback to the manager during the formal evaluation process.

Even if performance measurement and feedback are present, goal-setting will not be effective if employees are not committed to the organization's goals. Many of the leadership functions discussed in earlier chapters of this book are important sources of goal commitment. Inspiring through vision, role modeling, using legitimate authority, building self-confidence, and delegating responsibility all help promote commitment to organizational and personal goals.

Employees are also motivated by their own bottom line—namely, "What will happen to me if I buy into or reject these goals?" They weigh the potential rewards and punishments.

Rewarding and punishing are important factors in motivating followers to implement a leader's vision. Even followers who feel competent and capable of achieving the organization's vision will not continue to translate their readiness into action unless at some point they receive rewards from their leader.

Effective leaders typically reward employees for progress made toward the goals of the organization as a way of perpetuating that progress (Bass 1985; Kouzes and Posner 1987; Yukl 1989). If a leader gives a service award to an employee who meets the organization's goal of treating customers very well, for example, that employee as well as other employees should be more likely to treat customers in the same manner.

Roger Enrico of PepsiCo illustrates the importance of reward-allocation to organizations when he says that "treating the people well who produce is cheaper than having a big bureaucracy following them around trying to keep down costs" (quoted in Dumaine 1989, p. 86).

Effective leaders determine what is important to them and to the organization, and they allocate rewards accordingly. A reward system signals to others what the organization considers to be important values and appropriate behaviors (Kouzes and Posner 1987;

Peters 1987). Leaders must therefore design reward systems that are consistent with the organization's vision and accompanying goals. As Kouzes and Posner point out, "The grades or rewards that people receive or, equally important, do *not* receive tell them and others about what really counts in the organization" (1987, p. 205). Peters suggests that "well-constructed recognition settings provide the single most important opportunity to parade and reinforce the specific kinds of new behavior one hopes others will emulate" (1987, p. 370).

Peters illustrates the use of rewards for focusing followers' attention on certain organizational goals.

> If you want more cross-functional barrier-breaking . . . do what one insurance company did—at least 50 percent of each manager's awards for good performance went to those in other functions who helped his or her team. Likewise if you want to build team spirit . . . make sure that most of the awards go to teams of people, not [just to] individuals. (1987, p. 374–75)

Levi Strauss puts a heavy emphasis on how its managers manage in relation to actions that support and contribute to the company's stated aspirations (vision)—the "how" of management rather than the "what." One-third of a manager's raise, bonus, and other financial rewards depends on this ability to manage aspirationally. Managers know that their performance is judged from this perspective and that deficiencies are expected to be improved, no matter how many pairs of pants they are producing (Howard 1990).

The leadership role of reward-allocation also produces a motivated work force because of its empowering potential. Subordinates who feel empowered have leaders who "rewarded the achievements of their staffs by expressing personal praise and rewarding in highly visible and confidence-building ways" (Conger 1989, p. 19).

Empowerment should not be limited to white-collar workers. At Levi Strauss, 75 percent of the work force consists of operators in sewing and finishing plants. In the late 1980s, Levi Strauss initiated a "gain-sharing" experiment in its Blue Ridge, Georgia, plant. Workers were told that if they met predetermined production, absenteeism, and safety goals, the company would split fifty-fifty with them any savings that resulted from economies or productivity improvements. "They're taking initiatives and making things work better because it's in their interest and they don't have to be told," Haas reports. ". . . The most exciting thing is to see the transformation in the workplace. People who felt that they weren't valued despite twenty years of work for the company have a completely different attitude about their work" (Howard 1990, p. 142).

Empowering leaders use rewards to give their followers a sense that they have made a worthwhile contribution to the organization. Using rewards to empower followers is particularly critical when the goals of the organization are difficult to achieve. Conger finds that leaders in this situation have to "structure reward systems that would keep people 'pumped up'—that would ensure that their confidence and commitment would not be eroded by the pressures placed on them" (1989, p. 19).

Positive feedback does not have to wait until followers have achieved 100 percent of their long-term goals (Bass 1985). Rewarding effort and small steps taken toward reaching a goal is especially important for leaders who set challenging goals for their subordinates. By giving this feedback, leaders can empower their followers by setting challenging goals without causing them to be frustrated when the goals are not fully met.

The most effective leaders recognize subordinates' contributions to the achievement of a vision by using a wide variety of rewards— both tangible and nontangible. Tangible rewards include such things as pay, promotions, and bonuses. Motorola, for example, has rewarded employees who learned extra skills and improved quality with bonuses equal to 30 percent of their salaries (Hillkirk 1989). PepsiCo gives extensive tangible rewards—such as earnings, promotions, and company cars—to those employees who do well (Dumaine 1989).

Tangible rewards can serve as powerful motivators. Promotions send a strong message to employees about what the organization "wants here." If an innovative and risk-taking manager is promoted over a more conservative manager, other employees will recognize that the organization values innovation and individuals who are innovative. Salary increases and bonuses provide concrete signals that rewarded employees have performed effectively and have contributed to achieving the organization's vision and goals.

Nontangible rewards can give equally clear signals, can be greatly appreciated by subordinates, and can motivate employees to work toward achieving the organization's vision. Kouzes and Posner find that "although salary increases or bonuses are appreciated, individual's needs for and appreciation of rewards extends much further" (1987, p. 247). To praise and recognize employees' contributions, leaders use a wide variety of techniques, such as spending time with employees, sending thank-you notes, having lunch with employees, and running employee-of-the-month contests. In fact, Kouzes and Posner (1987) argue that the creative use of rewards often distinguishes leaders from managers.

Sam Preston, retired executive vice-president of S. C. Johnson Wax, exemplifies the creative use of rewards. Says one researcher, "He had a habit of sending little notes with a bold 'DWD' [damned well done] scrawled across the top, after coming across a sparkling effort" (Peters 1987, p. 371).

Sue Cook, a consultant at the Tom Peters Groups, gives out stickers, tee-shirts, and buttons and other awards when people achieve a milestone (Kouzes and Posner 1987). And "public praise and material rewards for workers who have gone out of their way for customers" were found to be the reward programs most popular with employees at American Express and other companies known for outstanding customer service (Davidow and Uttal 1989, p. 129).

The most successful leaders hold celebrations regularly that offer *both* tangible and nontangible rewards to their followers. Peters insists that leaders should "celebrate—informally and formally—the 'small wins' that are indicative of the solid day-to-day performance turned in by more than 90 percent of [the] work force" (1987, p. 366). Zaphiropoulos of Versatec supports that policy. He holds an annual spring celebration where two thousand managerial personnel receive bonuses. Zaphiropoulos believes that "if you are going to give someone a check, don't just mail it. Have a celebration" (quoted in Kouzes and Posner 1987, p. 12).

Domino's Pizza is another company that believes in the motivating potential of celebrations. Annually, the company holds an employee olympics, where participation ranges from the president of the company to the dough-makers. There, employees compete in various games for large cash prizes and vacations. The company's "investment," says one author, "has an invaluable return—honed skills plus a powerful sense of camaraderie and overall excitement that propels mostly young, inexperienced people through a system in which there is a great potential for stress" (Peters 1987, pp. 373–74).

To gain the benefits that are associated with rewarding followers, leaders must pay close attention to the manner in which they allocate rewards. Rewards should be tied both to goals and to performance (Bass 1985; Manz and Sims 1989). Kouzes and Posner (1987) suggest that tying rewards to performance entails the following principles:

- Make certain that people know what is expected of them.
- Provide feedback about performance.
- Reward only those who meet the standards [or who make good progress towards them].

Worthington Industries' approach is a good example of tying compensation to performance. Each quarter, the company distributes 17 percent of its pretax profits on the basis of divisional performance (Peters 1987). Tying rewards to performance is crucial if leaders want to get the behaviors that they desire or expect.

Effective leaders also recognize that rewards that recognize employee contributions to achieving the vision should be used on a regular basis. They take steps to ensure that every deserving person is rewarded in some way, regardless of how big or small his or her accomplishment.

Finally, leaders make the most effective use of rewards when they tailor them to the needs and expectations of their followers. Leaders must be sure the employees value whatever it is that they are being rewarded with. Such individualized consideration, described by Bass (1985), gives followers personal attention and recognizes that each individual is different. Once again, the critical leadership function of assessing followers comes into play here.

Self-reward is possible for some people, and its importance, especially for those who work toward self-set goals, is emphasized by Manz and Sims (1989). It can take the form of self-recognition and praise, self-satisfaction from attaining goals, and the pleasure involved in working on self-designed tasks. Self-generated rewards cannot completely take the place of rewards administered by leaders, however, and should be thought of as supplemental. People want to feel good about themselves and need to be recognized by others for their achievements by pay raises, promotions, and appropriate thanks.

Sometimes leaders must punish employees who are not behaving in line with the organization's vision and its accompanying goals. Punishments can range from pressure tactics to intimidation to termination. Motorola employees, for example, along with a possible 30 percent bonus, were also faced with possible penalties. Unacceptable product quality (in this case, electronic pagers containing five thousand defects per million parts) had to be improved (that is, reduced to five hundred defects or less), or the managers responsible would jeopardize their raises, their shot at promotion, or even their jobs (Hillkirk 1989, p. 28).

Punishment is most effective when managers

- tie the punishment clearly to the undesirable behavior, and
- provide feedback regarding why the individual was punished and the types of alternative behaviors that are expected. (Manz and Sims 1989)

Punishment should not be the dominant leadership technique, however, because research shows that positive reward is generally more effective than punishment in managing employee behavior in the long run (Manz and Sims 1989).

Managing Information

Managing information is related to many aspects of a leader's responsibility and activities, such as reviewing and monitoring feedback, planning, and decision-making. Gathering and processing information consumes a large proportion of a leader's time (Bass 1985; Kotter 1982, 1988). A leader must be skilled at gathering needed information and integrating it appropriately to make effective decisions, often under conditions of time pressure, uncertainty, and turbulence (Bass 1981; Cox and Cooper 1988; Gabarro 1987; Kotter 1982; Kouzes and Posner 1987).

Information-gathering is an essential facet of information management, and listening is a key method of gathering it (Gabarro 1987). Communication channels are the veins and arteries of new ideas. These channels are a crucial means of generating ideas for new products, processes, and services (Kouzes and Posner 1987).

Leaders must create an environment in which listening is cherished and opportunities for structured and unstructured listening are provided.

The leader is the model for an organization's responsive listening. Peters (1987) lists a number of factors that help leaders create a listening environment, which include

- creating a nonthreatening environment;
- creating a physical place to listen;
- remembering to listen and not preach;
- obtaining and/or providing training in listening;
- creating frequent opportunities for listening; and
- maintaining the proper attitude toward listening.

Leaders at all levels in an organization make a conscious effort to listen to their employees and to integrate and act on the information they receive. Leadership expert Ralph Stodgill concurs, saying that "open, easy, ready communications not only contribute to the extent the leader and the group can influence each other, but also the extent they will be effective" (1974, p. 468).

Leaders can facilitate information-gathering by practicing what has been termed "management by wandering around." This practice involves listening to and observing employees. Leaders who engage in this practice take advantage, on a daily basis, of the large pool of potentially fruitful sources of information in the organization. They leave their offices and make informal contact with various members of the organization in their work environments. Kouzes and Posner argue that "it is only through human contact that change and innovation can be effectively led. It does not happen from the 52nd floor in the headquarters building. Leaders stay in touch" (1987, p. 60). The key benefit of "wandering around" is that, as an information-gathering strategy, it provides a great opportunity to keep current with the newest information (Bass 1985).

"Wandering around" may seem unsystematic, but many leaders have found it to be a valuable source of knowledge. Renn Zaphiropoulos of Versatec finds this method to be particularly useful. He deliberately makes contact with his employees to gather information about their daily activities and the progress of his highly successful organization (Versatec 1979).

When Debi Coleman, former division operations manager for

Apple Computer, was attempting to increase the plant's performance, she made it a practice to listen to all employees to find out what was going on. To do this she spent "time on the floor . . . five hours a day" (Kouzes and Posner 1987, p. 6).

In another company, an employee remarked of his new superior: "One thing that was very important to me was his just spending a hell of a lot of time and listening to details. . . . He came down and became involved in understanding things his predecessor didn't have time for. . . . It's important to feel that you and your boss are talking on the same wavelength" (quoted in Gabarro 1987, p. 117). Listening and "wandering around" are important and easily implemented methods of obtaining information.

There are also more structured methods of information gathering. Kouzes and Posner (1987) suggest that leaders hold breakfast meetings or utilize suggestion boxes as additional methods of gaining internal information. Another readily available source of information is employee committees. As we have seen, when Stewart Bainum returned to Manor Care, his primary strategy for developing a vision was to talk with people. In addition to informal conversations, he formed a management committee and asked, "What's wrong, and what's right?" The information he received from that committee highlighted the problems existing in the corporation and made clear the need for a vision that emphasized top-quality patient care (Bainum 1989). More frequent use of meetings by general managers has been found to correlate with their success, in a study by Gabarro (1987).

When Intel Corporation became aware that its newly hired engineers, who were recent graduates, were more current on the latest technological advances than their executives were, it instituted formal meetings that provided opportunities for an exchange of information (Bass 1985). Since the company as a whole needed to keep current to be competitive in the marketplace, this interaction brought everybody up to speed—technologically. Being supportive of internal changes such as this is a method suggested by Hickman and Silva (1984) to improve or develop a leader's vision.

A leader can receive a large amount of information from inside the organization through the formalized management-information systems that are already in place. Company records can give a manager internal-performance information about what is not working or what can be improved. Kouzes and Posner (1987) advise managers to go find something to fix rather than wait for problems to develop from whatever is in functional disrepair.

The external environment is still another important source of information for formulating a vision and successful product and service strategies. Rapidly forming trends and changes in an industry quickly leave the inattentive leader behind. By constant reading, by attending conferences and lectures, and by talking with industry experts and customers, leaders can become aware of the changes in the environment in which they function and of how they can expect their organizations to be affected by them. George Hatsopoulos of Thermo Electron remarked in an interview for *Inc.* magazine, "The more you understand the overall environment . . . the better able you'll be able to find the [profitable] opportunities" (quoted in Posner and Solomon 1988, p. 36).

Networking has become an annoying buzzword to some professionals, but it is nonetheless an invaluable tool for gathering information from the external environment. Developing and maintaining contact with individuals outside the organization who are important sources of information has become essential to organizational survival. Haas at Levi Strauss attributes his company's success to practices such as making a real effort to listen to suppliers and customers, as well as to people within the organization (Howard 1990).

The network of relationships for general managers consists of hundreds of people both inside and outside their organizations (Kotter 1982). Successful leaders are especially adept at networking. Hatsopoulos is known for his networking abilities and activities, which he claims are responsible for allowing his organization to anticipate and meet future needs in the industry. He makes a concerted effort to gather information by keeping in touch with members of Congress, government agencies, and other companies in his industry. He also researches relevant topics by doing extensive reading on his own (Posner and Solomon 1988).

The other side of the information coin is *information dissemination*. It, too, is used extensively by effective leaders. CEO Max DePree of Herman Miller identifies a crucial function of leader communications as passing along values to newly hired members and reaffirming those values among existing members. He argues, "A corporation's values are its lifeblood. Without effective communication, actively practiced, without the art of scrutiny, those values will disappear in a sea of trivial memos and impertinent reports" (DePree 1989, p. 95). A leader must also ensure that employees have the information they need to accomplish their goals. Dissemination of information gains its importance from the impact it has on the effective use of power in an organization. As William G. McGowan, chairman and CEO of MCI, states:

> In the preceding era, power always rested with the hoarders of information, usually middle managers operating precisely between data sources and decision-makers. Suddenly, the hoarders are gone, slashed away, and information is wholly within the public realm. Who now holds the power? Those who share the data and make decisions from the data. Information is unique among all commodities in that its value comes from sharing. In the successful information-based structure, sharing takes place horizontally as well as vertically (personal communication).

Some leaders hoard information in an attempt to enhance their power or to hide their problems or past mistakes. But hoarding information can lead to long-term problems—particularly today, when errors need to be corrected quickly, not hidden, to retain a competitive position. Further, leaders who hoard information are not considered trustworthy; sharing information, by contrast, helps build employees' trust.

When information is readily available to employees and managers, they have better knowledge of what actions need to be taken. One true source of power for leaders, then, is in organizing an information-based structure so that gathered information can be quickly dispersed to those who can put it to the best use.

Disseminating information throughout an organization has a number of benefits. Sharing information empowers followers to excel in their performance by giving them a resource they need in order to succeed (Kouzes and Posner 1987). With information, managers can make informed decisions and understand the ramifications of those decisions for the organization. Sharing information increases employee capabilities for problem-solving.

Shared information can also motivate employees. Everett J. Suters, CEO of a small company, was surprised to discover that simply by informing managers of the company finances, they became motivate because they felt important. He remarks, "If my experience is any guide, you'll discover that the more open you are, the more responsibility your people will take on. And the more committed they'll feel to you and your organization" (Suters 1987, p. 112).

For leaders to maintain a high level of motivation in their followers, it is essential that the largest possible number of individuals within a system feel that they share ownership of the problem, and that they themselves are part of the solution (Gardner 1986–88).

In addition to dispersing information inside an organization, effective leaders also motivate their followers by serving as their spokesperson to external constituencies such as customers, competitors, the government, and regulatory agencies. In speaking for the organization, an effective leader represents the members' values, efforts, and concerns. This spokesperson role, as identified by Mintzberg (1973), motivates employees by creating a source of organizational unity. A leader should recognize the importance of this outside role—as lobbyist or public-relations representative to outside constituents—to the internal organization.

Information dissemination also has its pitfalls; there are points of diminishing return that must be identified. The amount of paperwork and pieces of information that employees must deal with can become too great (Tichy and Devanna 1986). A computer at GE, for example, used to spit out seven daily reports, one of which alone made a stack of paper twelve feet high. This only served to overwhelm top executives with useless information. After GE reduced the amount of information the executives received, the remaining data were utilized much more effectively (Sherman 1989).

Leaders can help to improve information flow by effectively reducing the amount of unnecessary and unimportant information. PepsiCo, for one, is decreasing the amount of paper-shuffling by instituting policies that encourage writing one-page memos and making phone calls rather than writing lengthy reports (Dumaine 1989).

Decreasing unneeded information can increase organizational flexibility and responsiveness to environmental changes and help increase employee motivation (Tichy and Devanna 1986).

Team-Building

Leaders who are skillful at building cooperative teams increase the likelihood that their subordinates will pull together to implement the organizational vision (Gabarro 1987; Hambrick 1987). The ability to build cohesive management teams is so crucial that, according to at least one study, it distinguishes successful leaders from unsuccessful ones (Gabarro 1987). Cohesive work teams are necessary because a shared vision does not—by itself—ensure that individuals will work well together. Even the most enthusiastic and talented followers cannot get extraordinary things done unless they work together effectively; "Fostering collaboration . . . is the key leaders use to unlock the energies and talents available in the organization" (Kouzes and Posner 1987, p. 135).

Cooperative teams also provide support to subordinates who may face obstacles and challenges during the long journey toward realizing the corporate vision. Kouzes and Posner therefore recommend "building strong social and interpersonal ties within the project team" (1987, p. 231).

Leaders employ a number of techniques to foster the kind of trust and collaboration necessary to ensure that individuals work together as an effective team. Practical strategies include

- creating cooperative goals that can only be reached by individuals who work together;
- making use of project teams, task forces, and problem-solving committees; and
- implementing [partially] group-based reward systems. (Kouzes and Posner 1987)

Building cohesive teams must start with top management because the performance of an organization is greatly dependent on the quality of management at that level (Hambrick 1987; Smith and Harrison 1986). Says one researcher, "The amounts of open-mindedness, perseverance, communication skills, vision, and other key characteristics that exist within the team clearly set the limits for how well the team—and, in turn, the firm—can operate" (Hambrick 1987, p. 2).

In the process of building an effective top-management team, Columbia University professor Don Hambrick (1987) argues, leaders must spend considerable time in assessing—and then narrowing—the gap between the skills, knowledge, and values that currently exist among the members of their team, on the one hand, and those required to effectively implement the vision, on the other. Leaders can narrow that gap by taking some of the following actions:

- training managers in the skills and knowledge they lack;
- replacing managers who do not share the organization's values; and
- hiring managers who have expertise in areas not covered by the management team.

In addition to ensuring that individuals in a top-management team work well together, leaders should assess team members and make the most effective use of their managerial talents. Managers in the team can be assigned the roles in which they are known to function most effectively. This effective delegation may allow the leader to provide the vision, for example, while other team members may set the agenda and perform short-term implementation activities.

A top-management team also can be used to compensate for the leader's weaknesses. Leaders skillful at building teams do not have to be good at everything to enable extraordinary things to happen in their organization, because "the best leader is one who ensures that the appropriate talent and skill is built into the team" (Gardner 1986–88, p. 16).

Promoting Change, Innovation, and Risk-Taking

An effective leader initiates and fosters change and innovation (Bennis and Nanus 1985; Burns 1978; Cox and Cooper 1988; Gabarro 1987; Kouzes and Posner 1987; Peters 1987; Tichy and Devanna 1986). According to Peters, the job of a leader is "to prepare people and organizations to deal with—to love, to develop affection for—change" (1987, p. 468).

Change comes in many different forms. It may take the form of new products and services, new markets, technical innovations, or improved quality of products and services. Whatever form change takes, it is clear that a leader's ability to create and manage change is crucial not only to achieving the vision but to the success and survival of the organization.

Innovations must be constantly "proposed, tested, rejected, modified, and adopted" for organizations to be effective (Peters 1987, p. 468). Successful companies such as Wal-Mart pride themselves on their ability to change. Referring to the future of the Wal-Mart corporation, its executives state that "the only thing constant at Wal-Mart is change" (Huey 1989, p. 61).

Due to the ever-changing business environment, change must occur quickly. In "The Winning Organization," Jeremy Main (1988) states that in the current world economy, change must be made with speed in order for an organization to remain competitive. The ability to change more rapidly is an advantage that new, smaller companies often have over corporate giants.

The situation faced by Bank of America illustrates the need for change in order to react to and survive in the ever-changing environment (Clausen 1989). A. W. Clausen vacated his spot as chairman of the highly successful Bank of America, but when he returned just five years later, he found that the bank was losing money and that there were serious questions about its ability to survive. In a speech to MBA students at the University of California, Los Angeles, Clausen stated that the reason for the bank's problems was that the world had changed and the bank had not responded rapidly enough to the new challenges thrust upon it by deregulation. Clausen set to work on the problem, and within three years, he had turned the bank around.

Clausen suggests that in times of change the conventional wisdom is frequently wrong. Instead of relying on old responses, leaders must make realistic appraisals of the current situation, then develop an appropriate and immediate course of action. This may necessitate creating new and fresh strategies or even restructuring the organization to assure its success.

Implementing change in an organization is described by Tichy and Devanna (1986) as a multistep process, involving

- recognizing the need for change;
- creating a vision geared toward change; and
- institutionalizing the changes.

This process must be a continual one. Lee Iacocca, for instance, recognized the need for change when he faced the crisis at Chrysler. He developed a vision that would facilitate changes as an ongoing procedure at Chrysler as part of its search for success.

Making effective change often requires utilizing an incremental process in which big problems requiring big solutions are broken down into small, achievable steps (Kouzes and Posner 1987). This allows followers to experience a number of small wins so that the enormity of the required change doesn't become overwhelming to them. Starting this process with actions under the leader's control—to get the ball rolling—then building upon those actions with the actions of others is an effective way to initiate major change (Kouzes and Posner 1987) and helps assure it will occur successfully in an organization.

No matter what strategies are employed, any change that occurs must start with the organization's vision. The vision must be one that allows for and encourages change, even though it remains constant. The vision must "encourage continual risk-taking and failing, or else the continual testing and stretching and enhancing—changing—of everything will not occur." This requires a vision that "not only inspires, ennobles, empowers, and challenges, but at the same time provokes . . . people to take day-to-day risks involved in testing and adapting and extending the vision." It must be specific enough to guide employees in their course of direction yet "general enough to leave room for the taking of bold initiatives in today's ever-changing environment" (Peters 1987, pp. 478, 485, 482).

A number of corporate visions fulfill the dual purpose of providing employees with the overarching direction of the organization and of leaving room for initiative and innovation. The founder of Federal Express, Fred Smith, had a vision of a reliable, quick mail service. Apple Computer founder Steve Jobs wanted to create a computer for the average person. These visions were crucial in bringing about change and, in turn, success for their organizations.

Beyond the vision, there are a number of ways by which leaders bring about change in their organizations. These include

- creating "strategic" visions;
- building a selection system that hires persons oriented toward change and innovation;
- developing new goal systems aimed at change;

- revamping the reward systems; and
- restructuring the organization.

Firms such as 3M, PepsiCo, and Citicorp are constantly reorganizing, while less-successful companies choose to restructure only every half-dozen years. Peters insists that "if you aren't reorganizing, pretty substantially, once every six to twelve months, you're probably out of step with the times" (1987, p. 564).

Leaders should actually set quantitative innovation goals for their followers; goals that allow innovation to be measured. To do this, a leader must define what constitutes an innovation, set goals for the achievement of innovation, then involve everyone in the innovation process. Innovation, in short, must become a way of life.

A dynamic leader can be thwarted by passive followers. Thus, leaders must evaluate and reward employees according to their ability to create change. A vice-president at IBM who champions change comments that the question—What have you changed?—has become the most frequent query at all levels throughout his firm. If the employees of a company are not creating change, they are impeding the success of the organization.

Although making any change involves risk, taking risks is essential in order to be successful. Kouzes and Posner (1987) encourage leaders to experiment and take risks (as well as encouraging others to do the same) because taking risks is identified as one of the keys to effective business leadership.

The possibility of failure is inherent in risk-taking. But to truly promote creativity and gain its benefits, a leader must be willing to accept occasional failure as a learning experience. A leader must even reward intelligent failures by employees in order to encourage them to take risks when they are striving toward innovation and change (Peters 1987). Otherwise, employees will be inhibited and may not risk making an error. Kouzes and Posner explain that "it is easier for people to say yes (to change) when you can minimize the costs of their potential mistakes" (1987, p. 236).

Senior managers at Levi Strauss try to be explicit about their own vulnerability and failings, reports CEO Haas. "We talk to people about the *bad* decisions we've made. It demystifies senior management and removes the stigma traditionally associated with taking risks" (Howard 1990, p. 139).

Promoting change *is* risky, but the overall benefits from successes should far outweigh the costs of failure. Only through change can successful organizations be created and sustained.

Summary

Implementation of the corporate vision is central is successful leadership and requires the development of an agenda of tasks to be accomplished. These include structuring the organization in ways that decrease excessive bureaucracy; selecting, acculturating, and training employees so that they possess the needed skills and values; motivating them to produce results; assembling them into teams of individuals who can work together effectively; managing the gathering and dissemination of information; and initiating and fostering change and innovation to assure the organization's survival.

6

A Case Study

Implementing Leadership for Quality—The
Room Air Conditioner Industry

Despite the numerous examples used in the preceding commentary on leadership, the concepts may still seem rather abstract. Although we have discussed the basic requirements for and principles of leadership, we have not explicitly shown how these ideas can be applied to or implemented in a specific situation.

Fortunately, the brilliant work of David Garvin (1983, 1988) of the Harvard Business School provides just such an illustration. Garvin has conducted an intensive six-year study of nine U.S. and seven Japanese companies that manufacture room air conditioners. As a group, these companies controlled 90 percent of the market in the two countries. Although his study was not designed to focus on leadership, many of his observations are relevant to the subject. Garvin found that the U.S. manufacturers differed markedly among themselves in the quality of their products and, furthermore, that the best-quality U.S. manufacturers achieved a lower average quality than the worst-quality Japanese manufacturers. Garvin's study identified the reasons for these quality differences.

Significantly, Garvin did not attribute the quality differences between the U.S. and Japanese plants to such commonly publicized factors as plant layout or degree of automation or cultural differences in employee loyalty. Rather, he attributed the differences to a difference in company philosophies and their implementation—factors that are within the control of leaders and managers.

Since Garvin was not concerned with leadership traits and skills, we will start by discussing what he said generally about vision. Of the Japanese companies, Garvin wrote,

> The commitment [to quality] was deeply ingrained and clearly communicated. It was visible everywhere: in statements of company philosophy, policy manuals, and charts and banners on the wall. At Matsushita, for example, quality appeared prominently in the company's slogan [a vision statement?]: "Let us limitlessly supply good quality products. . . ." An even stronger directive came from the company's quality manual: "Quality must be the first preference in the [work] group." (1988, pp. 201–202)

As noted in earlier chapters, establishing a vision and a vision statement and communicating it is not enough. As one U.S. air conditioner executive put it, "I've been talking about quality, but obviously it hasn't gotten anywhere. Now we'll tell people what to do" (quoted in Garvin 1988, p. 170). It was only after the executive did so, by developing a specific and agenda, that quality began to improve.

What specific actions did the Japanese and/or the better U.S. manufacturers take in order to insure high-quality air conditioners? One action was to institute *training*. The training program of the Japanese assembly workers typically lasted six months; by contrast, most of the U.S. workers were trained for only a few hours or at best a few days. In short, the U.S. workers were trained just enough to go through the motions of doing the tasks, while the Japanese workers were, by most standards, overtrained. Further, the Japanese workers were trained not only in assembly but in techniques of statistical quality control. In U.S. plants, by contrast, it was usually only engineers who received statistical training.

Another specific action was *role modeling*. Some Japanese executives actually attended the quality-control training programs and even conducted some of the training themselves. The top executives of the better U.S. plants, too, were typically actively involved in quality meetings, and some talked to customers about problems as well.

The more effective plants made extensive use of *goal-setting*. The top managers would set annual quantitative goals for quality, such as goals limiting acceptable production-defect and failure rates for the product in the field. The three U.S. plants that set targets for reducing field failures, for example, were the only ones to cut their service call rates by more than 25 percent. All the Japanese companies had companywide goals (Garvin 1983). These overarching goals were supported at each lower level by more specific goals. At the production or assembly level in Japanese plants, for instance, *goals would be set for every inspection point along the production line* (Garvin 1983). Goals would also be set for vendors, requiring that their components achieve a specified level of quality. Goal-setting was based on the *Kaizen* principle of constant improvements (Imai 1986).

Goal priorities for foremen and first-line supervisors were clearly specified. At four of the six Japanese plants from which ratings were obtained, supervisors believed that high quality was the top priority of the manufacturing department. At most of the U.S. plants, by contrast, meeting production schedules was rated the top priority. At the U.S. plants, the quality that was actually achieved rose according to how important the plant supervisors perceived quality to be.

The priority given to quality as a goal affected the type or number of quality *measurements* that were taken and, therefore, the type and amount of *feedback* that was provided to workers and managers. In the Japanese plants, defect rates were reviewed daily. In the best U.S. plants, rates were reviewed about every three days, and in the worst U.S. plants about every seven days. The Japanese measuring of vendor performance was far more extensive; they typically inspected 100 percent of the components for a new vendor. In some of the U.S. plants, the vendor components were not inspected at all. The Japanese had more inspectors on the assembly line and provided far more elaborate breakdowns of information than the American plants did. The Japanese, for example, would calculate defect rates for every part that was installed on the assembly line. The same standard applied to field repair work. "At one company," wrote Garvin, "repairmen had to submit reports on every defective unit they fixed. In general, it was not unusual for Japanese managers to be able to identify the thirty different ways in which Switch X had failed on Model Y during the last several years" (1983, p. 70).

Statistical quality control was used far more extensively and consistently in the Japanese plants than in those in the United States. The best U.S. plants, however, had more detailed feedback than the worst ones. The speed of receiving feedback from the field was also faster in the Japanese plants. They would get data from field repairmen within one week to one month after a repair was made, whereas the U.S. plants would get the same information only after one month to a year had passed. Further, the Japanese plants conducted far more detailed and time-consuming in-plant audits of finished products than did the U.S. plants.

It is thus clear that *information-gathering* was far more thorough and extensive in the Japanese plants than in the U.S. plants; this was also true of the better U.S. plants in comparison with the poorer ones. The same was true with respect to *information dissemination*. The Japanese sent information down to the worker level as well as up to the managerial level, whereas at the U.S. plants, information typically went only upward. The Japanese also gave vendors extensive feedback about their products and performance and even went to the vendors' plants to help them make product improvements.

The Japanese plants practiced companywide or total quality control (TQC). This means that information about quality was shared across all functional specialties. Everyone (sales, engineering, manufacturing, and production employees) was involved in product design. Further, customers' opinions would be solicited since engineers' and manufacturing specialists' definitions of quality do not always correspond to those of customers.

In the Japanese plants, the reward system supported the quest for quality. *Rewards and performance evaluations* were based more on quality than on quantity of output. In the best U.S. plants, quality was also rewarded, but in the worst ones, the main incentives were given for total output regardless of quality.

It is clear from Garvin's findings that achieving a vision of quality is not simply a matter of having or communicating that vision. It also requires taking actions to bring that vision into reality. As Garvin put it, "Superior quality is associated with well-defined management practices and not simply a supportive corporate culture" (1988, p. 157). These well-defined management practices involve not just slogans but numerous, complex, time-consuming, and painstaking day-to-day activities that touch every activity of every employee. They do not involve single grandstand actions but thousands and thousands of small actions taken over and over, all directed to a single end. The overarching goal or vision directs and unifies these actions and gives them purpose, but it is the actions themselves that bring about the end result.

It is this integration of thought and action that makes possible the production not only of quality goods but of every productive human achievement. And it is leaders who are the driving force behind such thought and its implementation in action by organizations.

References

Ackoff, R. 1978. *The Art of Problem Solving*. New York: Wiley.

Bainum, S. 1989. Presentation to leadership class. (May 11).

Bass, B. M. 1981. *Handbook of Leadership: A Survey of Theory and Research*. New York: Free Press.

Bass, B. M. 1985. *Leadership and Performance beyond Expectations*. New York: Free Press.

Bass, B. M. 1990. *Handbook of Leadership*. New York: Free Press.

"Behind the Scenes at the Fall of Rolm." 1989. *Business Week* (July 10), 82–84.

Bennis, W. G., and B. Nanus. 1985. *Leaders: The Strategies for Taking Charge*. New York: Harper and Row.

Bentz, V. J. 1967. "The Sears Experience in the Investigation, Description, and Prediction of Executive Behavior." In F. R. Wickert and D. E. McFarland, eds., *Measuring Executive Effectiveness*. New York: Appleton-Century-Crofts.

Boyatzis, R. E. 1982. *The Competent Manager*. New York: Wiley.

Bray, D. W., R. J. Campbell, and D. L. Grant. 1974. *Formative Years in Business: A Long-Term AT&T Study of Managerial Lives*. New York: Wiley.

Burns, J. M. 1978. *Leadership*. New York: Harper and Row.

Burnside, R. M. 1988. "Encouragement as the Elixir of Innovation." *Issues and Observations* 8(3), 1–6. Greensboro, N.C.: Center for Creative Leadership.

Calonius, E. 1990. "America's Toughest Papermaker." *Fortune,* February 26, 80–83.

Clausen, A. W. 1989. "Principles for Managing Change." *AGSM Today,* Anderson Graduate School of Management at UCLA, (Summer), 4.

"Coming of Age: How the Events of the Past Decade Have Changed the Way We Think about Business." 1989. *Inc.* (April), 36–45.

Conger, J. A. 1988. *Charismatic Leadership: The Elusive Factor in Organizational Effectiveness*. San Francisco, Calif.: Jossey-Bass.

Conger, J. A. 1989. "Leadership: The Art of Empowering Others." *Academy of Management Executive* 3, 17–24.

Conger, J. A., and R. N. Kanungo. 1987. "Toward a Behavioral Theory of Charismatic Leadership in Organizational Settings." *Academy of Management Review* 12, 637–47.

Cox, C. J., and C. L. Cooper. 1988. *High Flyers: An Anatomy of Managerial Success*. Oxford: Basil Blackwell.

Davidow, W. H., and B. Uttal. 1989. *Total Customer Service*. New York: Harper and Row.

De La Croix, R. 1962. *John Paul Jones*. Translated from French by Edward Fitzgerald. London: Frederick Muller.

Dumaine, B. 1989. "Those Highflying PepsiCo Managers." *Fortune* (April 10), 78–86.

Dunnette, M. D. 1971. "Multiple Assessment Procedures in Identifying and Developing Managerial Talent." In P. McReynolds, ed., *Advances in Psychological Assessment*, vol. 2. Palo Alto, Calif.: Science and Behavior Books.

DePree, M. 1989. *Leadership Is an Art*. New York: Doubleday.

Eden, D. 1990. *Pygmalion in Management*. Lexington, Mass.: Lexington Books.

Farnham, A. 1989. "The Trust Gap." *Fortune* (December 4), 56ff.

Fiedler, F. E., and J. E. Garcia. 1987. *New Approaches to Effective Leadership: Cognitive Resources and Organizational Performance*. New York: Wiley

Fisher, C. D., and E. A. Locke. In Press. "The New Look in Job Satisfaction Research and Theory." In C. J. Cranny, P. C. Smith, and E. F. Stone, eds. *Job Satisfaction: Advances in Research and Application*. Lexington, Mass.: Lexington Books.

Friedman, H. S., L. M. Prince, R. E. Riggio, and M. R. DiMatteo. 1980. "Understanding and Assessing Nonverbal Expressiveness: The Affective Communication Test." *Journal of Personality and Social Psychology* 39, 333–51.

Gabarro, J. J. 1987. *The Dynamics of Taking Charge*. Boston, Mass.: Harvard Business School Press.

Garvin, D. A. 1983. "Quality on the Line." *Harvard Business Review* (September–October), 65–75.

Garvin, D. A. 1988. *Managing Quality*. New York: Free Press.

Gardner, J. W. 1986–88. *Leadership Papers*, vols. 1–11. Washington, DC: Independent Sector.

Gardner, J. W. 1989. "Leaders and Hidden Energies." *Aspen Quarterly* (Fall).

Gendron, G., and B. Burlingham. 1989. "Thriving on Order." *Inc.* (December), 47ff.

Girard, K. F. 1989. "To the Manor Born." *Warfield's* (March), 68–75.

Gordon, T. 1977. *Leader Effectiveness Training, L.E.T.: The No-Lose Way to Release the Productive Potential of People*. New York: Wyden Books.

Gorman, C. 1989. "Smooth Operation." *Time* (September 18), 60–61.

Hackman, J. R., and G. R. Oldham. 1976. "Motivation through the Design of Work: Test of a Theory." *Organizational Behavior and Human Performance* 16, 250–79.

Hambrick, D. C. 1987. "The Top Management Team: Key to Strategic Success." *California Management Review* 30(11), 1–20.

Hickman, H. C., and M. A. Silva. 1984. *Creating Excellence: Managing Corporate Culture, Strategy, and Change in the New Age*. New York: New American Library.

Hillkirk, J. 1989. "Top Quality Is Behind Comeback." *USA Today* (March 28), 1B–2B.

House, R. J. 1988. "Power and Personality in Complex Organizations." In L. L. Cummings and B. M. Staw, eds., *Research in Organizational Behavior* 10. Greenwich, Conn.: JAI Press.

House, R. J. 1989. "Charismatic Leadership: Theory and Research." Presentation at University of Maryland, College Park (April 7).

House, R. J., and M. L. Baetz. 1979. "Leadership: Some Empirical Generalizations and New Research." In B. M. Staw, ed., *Research in Organizational Behavior* 1. Greenwich, Conn.: JAI Press.

House, R. J., J. Woycke, and E. M. Fodor. 1987. "Motive Patterns, Perceived Behavior, and Effectiveness of Charismatic and Noncharismatic U.S. Presidents." University of Toronto, unpublished manuscript.

Howard, A., and D. W. Bray. 1988. *Managerial Lives in Transition: Advancing Age and Changing Times.* New York: Guilford Press.

Howard, A. 1990. "Values Make the Company: An Interview with Robert Haas." *Harvard Business Review* (September–October), 133–44.

Howell, J. M., and P. J. Frost. 1989. "A Laboratory Study of Charismatic Leadership." *Organizational Behavior and Human Decision Processes* 43, 243–69.

Howell, J. 1988. "Two Faces of Charisma." In J. Conger and R. Kunungo, eds., *Charismatic Leadership.* San Francisco, Calif.: Jossey-Bass.

Huey, J. 1989. "Wal-Mart: Will It Take Over the World?" *Fortune* (January 30), 52–59.

Imai, M. 1986. *Kaizen: The Key to Japan's Competitive Success.* New York: Random House.

Kaplan, R. E., and M. S. Mazique. 1983. *Trade Routes: The Manager's Network of Relationships* (Report No. 22). Greensboro, N.C.: Center for Creative Leadership.

Kepner, C. H., and B. B. Tregoe. 1981. *The New Rational Manager.* Princeton: Princeton Research Press.

Kotter, J. P. 1982. *The General Managers.* New York: Free Press.

Kotter, J. P. 1985. *Power and Influence.* New York: Free Press.

Kotter, J. P. 1988. *The Leadership Factor.* New York: Free Press.

Kotter, J. P. 1990. *A Force for Change.* New York: Free Press.

Kouzes, J. M., and B. Z. Posner. 1987. *The Leadership Challenge: How to Get Extraordinary Things Done in Organizations.* San Francisco, Calif.: Jossey-Bass.

Labich, K. 1988. "The Seven Keys to Business Leadership." *Fortune* (October 24), 58–66.

Locke, E. A., and G. P. Latham. 1984. *Goal Setting: A Motivational Technique That Works.* Englewood Cliffs, N.J.: Prentice Hall.

Locke, E. A., and G. P. Latham. 1990. *A Theory of Goal Setting and Task Performance.* Englewood Cliffs, N.J.: Prentice Hall.

Locke, E. A., D. Sirota, and A. D. Wolfson. 1976. "An Experimental Case Study of the Successes and Failures of Job Enrichment in a Government Agency." *Journal of Applied Psychology* 61, 701–11.

Lorange, P., and R. V. Vancil. 1977. *Strategic Planning Systems.* Englewood Cliffs, N.J.: Prentice Hall.

Lord, R. G., C. L. De Vader, and G. M. Alliger. 1986. "A Metaanalysis of the Relation between Personality Traits and Leadership Perceptions: An Application of Validity Generalization Procedures." *Journal of Applied Psychology* 71, 402–10.

Maddi, S. R., and S. C. Kobasa. 1984. *The Hardy Executive: Health under Stress.* Chicago: Dorsey Professional Books.

Main, J. 1988. "The Winning Organization." *Fortune* (September), 50–60.

Manz, C., and H. Sims. 1989. *SuperLeadership.* Englewood Cliffs, N.J.: Prentice Hall.

McCall, M. W., Jr., and M. M. Lombardo. 1983. *Off the Track: Why and How Successful Executives Get Derailed.* (Technical Report No. 21). Greensboro, N.C.: Center for Creative Leadership.

McClelland, D. C. 1965. "N-achievement and Entrepreneurship: A Longitudinal Study." *Journal of Personality and Social Psychology* 1, 389–92.

McClelland, D. C., and D. H. Burnham. 1976. "Power Is the Great Motivator." *Harvard Business Review* (March–April), 100–10.

Miner, J. B. 1978. "Twenty Years of Research on Role-Motivation Theory of Managerial Effectiveness." *Personnel Psychology* 31, 739–60.

Mintzberg, H. 1973. *The Nature of Managerial Work.* New York: Harper and Row.

Munsey, C. 1990. "Perot to Mids: Follow Academy's Rules." In *The Capitol* [Annapolis, Md.], (November 28), C–1.

Pearson, A. E. 1989. "Six Basics for General Managers." *Harvard Business Review* (July–August), 94–101.

Peters, T. 1987. *Thriving on Chaos: Handbook for a Management Revolution.* New York: Harper and Row.

Peters, T. 1989. "Doubting Thomas." *Inc.* (April), 82–92.

Posner, B. Z., and S. D. Solomon. 1988. "The Thinking Man's CEO." *Inc.* (November), 28–42.

Rand, A. 1961. *For the New Intellectual.* New York: Signet.

Schein, E. H. 1985. *Organizational Culture and Leadership.* San Francisco, Calif.: Jossey-Bass.

Schneider, B. 1987. "The People Make the Place." *Personnel Psychology* 40, 437–54.

Schneider, B., and A. E. Reichers. 1983. "On the Etiology of Climates." *Personnel Psychology* 36, 19–39.

Schriesheim, C. A., J. M. Tolliver, and O. C. Behling. 1983. "Leadership Theory: Some Implications for Managers." In A. D. Szilagyi, Jr., and M. J. Wallace, Jr., eds., *Readings in Organizational Behavior and Performance.* 3rd ed. Glenview, Ill.: Scott, Foresman.

Sherman, S. P. 1989. "The Mind of Jack Welch." *Fortune* (March 27), 39–50.

Smith, K. G., and J. K. Harrison. 1986. "In Search of Excellent Leaders." In W. D. Guth, ed., *The Handbook of Strategy*. New York: Warren, Gorham, and Lamont.

Srivastva, S., and Associates. 1986. *Executive Power*. San Francisco, Calif.: Jossey-Bass.

Steiner, G. A. 1969. *Top Management Planning*. New York: Macmillan.

Stogdill, R. M. 1974. *Handbook of Leadership*. New York: Free Press.

Suters, E. J. 1987. "Managing People: Show and Tell." *Inc.* (April), 111–12.

"Thriving on Order." 1989. *Inc.* [Interview with Steve Bostic] 11(12), 47ff.

Tichy, N. M., and M. A. Devanna. 1986. *The Transformational Leader*. New York: Wiley.

Umstot, D. D., C. H. Bell, and T. R. Mitchell. 1976. "Effects of Job Enrichment and Task Goals on Satisfaction and Productivity: Implications for Job Design." *Journal of Applied Psychology* 61, 379–94.

Versatec. 1979. *A Day with Renn Zaphiropoulos*. Harvard Business School Video.

Vroom, V. H., and A. G. Jago. 1988. *The New Leadership: Managing Participation in Organizations*. Englewood Cliffs, N.J.: Prentice Hall.

Wexley, K. N., and G. A. Yukl. 1984. *Organizational Behavior and Personnel Psychology*. 2d ed. Homewood, Ill.: Irwin.

Wheeler, D. J., and I. L. Janis. 1980. *A Practical Guide for Making Decisions*. New York: Free Press.

Yukl, G. A. 1981. *Leadership in Organizations*. Englewood Cliffs, N.J.: Prentice Hall.

Yukl, G. A. 1989. *Leadership in Organizations*. 2d ed. Englewood Cliffs, N.J.: Prentice Hall.

Zaleznik, A. 1989. *The Managerial Mystique*. New York: Harper and Row.

Index

About the
Authors

Edwin A. Locke is a professor of business and management and of psychology and chairman of the Management and Organization Faculty of the College of Business and Management at the University of Maryland. He received his undergraduate degree from Harvard University and his M.A. and Ph.D. in industrial psychology from Cornell University.

Locke is an internationally known behavioral scientist, whose work is included in leading textbooks and acknowledged in books on the history of management. He has published over 140 books, chapters, and articles that explore areas such as goal setting, work motivation, job satisfaction, incentives, and the philosophy of science. He is the author of *A Guide to Effective Study* (Springer, 1975); "The Nature and Causes of Job Satisfaction," in M. D. Dunnette's *Handbook of Industrial and Organizational Psychology* (Rand McNally, 1976); *Goal Setting: A Motivational Technique That Works* (Prentice Hall, 1984, with G. Latham); *Generalizing from Laboratory to Field Settings* (Lexington Books, 1986); and *A Theory of Goal Setting and Task Performance* (Prentice Hall, 1990, with G. Latham).

Locke has been elected a Fellow of the American Psychological Association, the Academy of Management, and the American Psychological Society, and is a member of the New York Academy of Sciences and the Society for Organizational Behavior. He was named a winner of the Outstanding Teacher-Scholar Award for the College Park campus during 1983–84 and of a division of the Behavioral and Social Sciences Teaching Award in 1985.

Locke has worked for and served as a consultant to several behavioral science research firms, consulting firms, and private organizations, and has also given talks before numerous business and professional groups.

Jill Wheeler, Jodi Schneider, Kathryn Niles, and Harold Goldstein are doctoral students in the industrial-organizational psychology program at the University of Maryland, College Park.

Shelley Kirkpatrick and Dong-Ok Chah are doctoral students in the organizational behavior program at the College of Business and Management at the University of Maryland.

Kurt Welsh is a doctoral student in the marketing program at the College of Business and Management at the University of Maryland.